Customer Obsession

Your Roadmap to Profitable CRM

by

Ad Nederlof
President and CEO
Genesys Telecommunications Laboratories

and

Dr. Jon Anton
Purdue University
Center for Customer-Driven Quality

Content Editor
Dr. Natalie Petouhoff
BenchmarkPortal, Inc.

Business Navigation

Only two centuries ago, early explorers (adventurous business executives of those bygone days) were guided primarily with a compass and celestial navigation using reference points like the North Star. Today's busy executive also needs guidance systems with just-in-time business intelligence to navigate through the challenges of locating, recruiting, keeping, and growing profitable customers. The Anton Press provides this navigational system through practical, how-to-do-it books for the modern day business executive.

THE

ANTON PRESS

4th Edition Copyright © 2003 (11-Dec-03)

The Anton Press, Santa Maria, CA 93455
Used pursuant to license. All rights reserved.

ISBN 0-9719652-0-X

Library of Congress Cataloging-in-Publication Data

Nederlof, Ad.
  Customer obsession: your roadmap to profitable CRM / by Ad Nederlof and Jon Anton ; content editor Natalie Petouhoff.
      p. cm.
  ISBN 0-9719652-0-X (pbk. : alk. paper)
  1. Customer relations--Management. I. Anton, Jon. II. Petouhoff, Natalie L. III. Title.
  HF5415.5 .N43 2002

                                                    2002007865

Dedication

All of my knowledge around this subject is based on interaction with my customers and partners all over the world. That's why I'd like to dedicate this book to the thousands of customers and hundreds of partners in all different industries and countries. Without them, this book could not have been written.

Ad Nederlof

This book is dedicated to my wonderful wife, Suzanne, and my sons, Cassidy and Sean. Their understanding and patience with my long hours of "burning the midnight oil" to complete this book is greatly appreciated.

Dr. Jon Anton

Table of Contents

i

iii

List of Figures

List of Tables

ACKNOWLEDGEMENTS

A special thanks to Greg Shenkman and Alec Miloslavsky, founders of Genesys 11 years ago and pioneers in CTI. Besides the fact that we became close friends, I also learned a lot from them. I would also like to thank Fred Janssen, VP, Global Field Marketing, Keli O'Mara, my personal assistant, and Dana Dye, PR Manager, for all of their preparations and logistic work on top of their regular busy schedules. Last but not least, I'd like to thank the customers who were willing to share their experiences and stories with me.

Ad Nederlof

I wish to acknowledge three outstanding graduates from my program at Purdue University. They are Natalie Avery, Colleen Kifner, and Michelle Cline. These individuals have taken what they learned at Purdue and multiplied it 100-fold in the CRM marketplace as managers, thought leaders, and successful practitioners.

Lastly, I want to mention Father Gerald Walker who was my most important mentor and influential teacher, and without whom much of my educational achievements would not have been possible.

Dr. Jon Anton

We also wish to thank Mandy Schuldt, our production manager, and her team, including Susan Hampton, Debi Cloud, Helen Ann Thomas, and Gail Carver, for their very professional work in taking our numerous drafts of the manuscript, and transforming its many words, graphs, and tables into an attractive and readable book.

By

Ray Lane
General Partner
Kleiner Perkins Caufield & Byers

Many companies are struggling to come to grips with their own implementation of customer relationship management (CRM) systems. The constant barrage of information from solution providers, vendors, and system integrators is often optimistic, sometimes confusing, occasionally unrealistic, and definitely overwhelming.

Finally, here is a book that covers the complete "journey" of CRM implementation. Ad Nederlof and Dr. Jon Anton have done the near impossible: to position CRM in such a way that it makes practical sense to C-level executives. Beginning with the title of the book, "Customer Obsession," on through the last chapter, this book positions CRM for what it really is, namely, a complete change in corporate strategy, from the top down, that brings the customer into focus. The customer has many faces, and the question is "can you recognize your customer" with your current information technology systems in place? Many can not. After you read this book, you will definitely know where to begin.

In the past twenty years, we have witnessed several waves of technology improvement initiatives. These include such high-flyers as "business process re-engineering," "total quality management," "supply chain optimization" and, more recently, "business to business e-commerce." Each of these technology initiatives have had a profound impact on how we do business, but we are now in the midst of the most profound change of all, namely the migration from company-centric management to customer-centric management— more popularly known as CRM. This book makes many very important points regarding CRM. And, with the lessons learned from the last few years of CRM implementations, this book guides businesses as they make their next move.

Today many products are mere commodities that are difficult to differentiate through features, functions, quality, or price. The new mind-set is definitely toward customer service as a differentiator. In particular, the new focus is on giving customers easy access to mission-critical information. For this reason, we see the growing importance of the multi-channel customer "answer" center of today. In this book the answer center has been converted to the CRM center – an important difference in perception that has significant business impact.

With the emergence of e-business, customers can now contact companies through many channels including the telephone, e-mail, Web site, chat, VOIP, kiosk, FAX, wireless, and many more. Through these electronic "touchpoints," customers are selecting products based on a new feature, namely, the ease of "accessibility" to information before, during, and after a purchase. How to organize this multi-channel technology is very much the topic of this book.

In this book you will learn that with this new focus on "accessibility," executives will recognize the CRM center as a significant revenue generator, perhaps the surest investment they can make in getting new customers, retaining existing customers, enhancing customer value, and ultimately improving their bottom-line profits. I recommend "Customer Obsession" as mandatory reading for all executives associated with customer relationship management.

Figure 1.1. What happens to bad customer relationships?

Accessibility Is The Key

Being "obsessed" about building lasting customer relationships is what this book is all about. Our message is plain and simple. In this century, only those companies led by CEOs and executive teams who are driven by "customer obsession" will survive. All others will go out of business, or be absorbed and merged into companies that are infatuated with customer obsession.

In the past fifteen years, we have witnessed several waves of technology improvement initiatives. We all remember major efforts in "business process reengineering," followed by "total quality management." Later, there was the "Y2K" impact. It is fair to say that each of these major technology improvement initiatives has had a profound impact on businesses by reducing product costs, adding new features, and improving product quality.

Today, however, global competition has reduced many products to mere commodities that are difficult to differentiate through features,

1

functions, quality, or price. Having reached parity, where price and quality are the "table stakes" of doing business, the paradigm shift is definitely toward being obsessed about customer service as a differentiator. In particular, the new focus is on giving customers easy "access" to mission-critical information—therefore, logically, the growing importance of the multi-channel customer relationship management (CRM) center of today.

With the emergence of e-business, customers can contact companies through many channels—including the telephone, e-mail, Web site, chat, VOIP, kiosk, FAX, wireless, and many more. Through these electronic "touchpoints," customers are selecting products based on a characteristic new to CRM, namely, the ease of "accessibility" to information about the product before, during, and after a purchase.

Because of this new focus on "accessibility," executives now recognize the CRM center as a significant generator of revenue, perhaps the surest investment they can make in attracting new customers, retaining existing customers, enhancing customer value, and ultimately improving their bottom-line profits.

With this newfound strategic importance of the customer "answer" center has come a vast array of emerging technology solutions to enable better customer service.

Figure 1.1 shows the dissatisfaction of a typical customer with the customer-company experience. It is our observation that:

- Customers don't like to repeat their names to a call center agent. The name should just be there on the agent's screen, right?

- Customers don't feel important when they are not rewarded for shopping.

- Customers don't like being transferred from person to person. They want their issues taken care of in one phone call.

- Customers don't like when you communicate with them using a method they do not prefer, e.g., some people like telephone calls and others like e-mail order confirmations.

- Customers don't like to be sold something they are not, and will never be, interested in.

So what is a CEO to do? Start by reading this book cover to cover, and then read it again. Give it to everyone on your team to read. And once you feel the team has mastered the basic concepts, then you and your company can begin the real journey of CRM, which starts with understanding the various definitions of CRM.

Definition of CRM

Let's begin with the "big picture" of customer relationship management (CRM) as shown in figure 1.2.

In this figure you can see that there are many different "customers" and, therefore, many customer relationships to manage. Also shown in figure 1.2 is how CRM is achieved by a focus on "continuous improvement" of all aspects of each relationship. This is achieved by the following three distinct activities:

1. A focus on improving the value of the product/service as perceived by the customer.

2. A focus on the recovery system that begins when something goes wrong.

3. A focus on competitive positioning through benchmarking to ensure that the customer is not lured away to a relationship with a competitor.

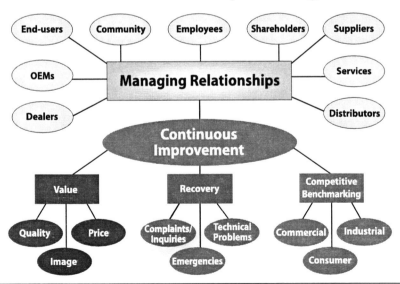

Figure 1.2. The interrelated aspects that, if included in the strategy, will return the investment of CRM

3

We see the achievement of CRM as more of a journey than a destination. "On the road to CRM," there are five high-level challenges that must eventually be met. These are:

1. Strategic CRM The team must begin by understanding the CEO's business strategy and then drive to create a holistic strategy for the CRM implementation.

2. Operational CRM You must build the technology infrastructure that can provide seamless accessibility by customers to mission-critical information about your products and services. The customer must have this access through all the standard channels, or "touchpoints," which include telephone, e-mail, Web chat, and a lot more. This process is often called **operational** CRM.

3. Analytical CRM At each customer touchpoint, you must strategically collect customer data "fingerprints," and then apply analytical tools to process this data into business intelligence to guide executive decision-making. In addition, this knowledge of each customer will allow you to further individualize future interactions with your customers. This process is often called **analytical** CRM.

4. Collaborative CRM Finally, for each customer, you must offer every possible alternative for self-directed service. In today's world of highly educated and discerning customers, the best customer service strategy is to offer customers every possible alternative to "help themselves." This process is often called **collaborative** CRM.

5. Supply Chain CRM No company can operate without its suppliers. Managing supplier relationships is equally important to the success of a company as managing their customers. This process is often called **supply chain** CRM.

These five challenges along the road to CRM implementation will be used as the guideposts in this book to help explain the various types of technology you will need as your customer solution grows over time.

In figure 1.3, we introduce the concept that all processes within a company, in fact, impact the customer. Yes, only "customer facing" processes actually "touch" the customer, but in fact, all processes within a company impact the customer's relationship with the

4

company. This is why each and every employee in a company must become obsessed with the customer, even when their day-to-day job is not directly interfacing with the customer. All jobs in a company impact the customer in the end.

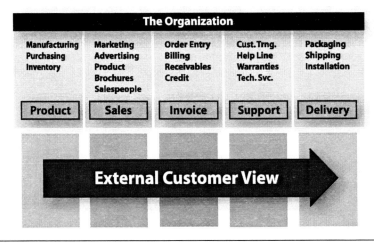

Figure 1.3. Processes that affect the customer

Analytical CRM measurement systems that can take raw data and turn it into management information are saving products, services, and customers. What we see is that a CRM measurement system can answer questions like the following:

- Why are customers upset?
- Which product/service has a problem?
- Which part of the world or country has the biggest concern?
- What is wrong with the product?
- Why are they not paying the bill? Are they unhappy?

The reason this kind of CRM data has so much impact is that a company's employees are enabled to quickly resolve the issue, and thus impact the customer relationship positively. When issues are resolved quickly—or even better—proactively caught, the company reaps the ROI for the CRM technology because they are serving the customer better. That positive impact increases the customer lifetime value (CLV), and that increase in CLV is what increases revenues and profits. The shift in thinking for the business world is to view *the CRM system as the "brain" with the intelligence that executives need to predict the future and stay ahead of it with factual information.*

Why measure? It seems there is no other choice. Companies that know how to measure customer satisfaction, customer lifetime value, and their CRM operations will be able to balance CRM technology expenditures and know *how good is good enough.*

Why CRM Is a Journey, Not a Destination

In today's fast moving and highly competitive market, products come and go. For companies large and small, the most important real asset, with measurable long-term value, is loyal, one-to-one customer relationships. A *fully implemented* CRM system provides executives with the ability to see the future and act on it to create loyal customers. It also provides an opportunity for them to learn about loyal customers and shift their company's strategy to service profitable customers better.

Prior to the creation of the mass marketing, outlet chain, mail order, e-commerce world that we live in today, individual proprietors created the ultimate CRM and loyal customers. They weren't equipped with multi-channel, data warehouse, and videoconference capabilities. What they did have were strong, personalized relationships with their customers. Creating the same customer relationship that was created in the "mom and pop" shops can be accomplished today with CRM solutions if there is a clear strategy, measuring technologies, improvement processes, and employees who excel at customer service.

The rise in expenditures for CRM is not surprising, given that top management is buying into CRM. The question is: Are they getting the return on the investment for the technology? Figure 1.4 shows the results of a survey of over 1,000 respondents when asked questions about their CRM implementation. The overall conclusion is that many are still looking for the real results from their investment. CRM software implementation led our list of reported improvement initiatives for call centers in 2000. Below are the answers to our benchmark questions related to measurable improvements following CRM implementation.

6

Status of CRM Improvement	Respondents
Regarding improved agent effectiveness:	
Agent effectiveness has greatly improved.	29%
Agent effectiveness is still to be determined.	59%
Agent effectiveness has not improve at all.	12%
Agent effectiveness is down.	0%
Regarding improved agent efficiency:	
Agent efficiency has greatly improved.	6%
Agent efficiency is still to be determined.	88%
Agent efficiency has not improve at all.	6%
Agent efficiency is down.	0%
Regarding increased sales:	
Sales per agent has greatly improved.	6%
Sales per agent is still to be determined.	53%
Sales per agent has not improve at all.	41%
Sales per agent is down.	0%
Regarding reduced after call work time:	
After call work time has greatly improved.	6%
After call work time is still to be determined.	53%
After call work time has not improve at all.	17%
After call work time has increased.	24%
Regarding improvements in call center reporting:	
Reporting has greatly improved.	24%
Reporting improvement is still to be determined.	76%
Reporting has not improve at all.	0%
Reporting now takes longer.	0%

©2001 Purdue University/BenchmarkPortal, Inc.

Figure 1.4. Survey results concerning CRM implementation

There is a delicate balance between the millions companies are investing in CRM systems versus the retention of highly profitable customers. The challenge an executive faces is knowing whether or not the money spent on CRM technology to foster the customer relationship is returning the investment the company expected or needed. Since customer relationship management is the main purpose of investing in the CRM technology, then it would make sense to measure how effective it is in cultivating the customer relationship. Yet many companies stop at implementing CRM systems and never make the connection that they need to measure how well it furthers the customer relationship to the point of creating more profits. Even further from implementation in most companies is taking those measurements and incorporating the results (the voice of their customers) into the company's business practices.

7

Ten Characteristics of World Class CRM Centers

Through our annual benchmarking studies of CRM centers, we have been able to select those centers that were truly better than the rest of the pack. We asked the managers of these world-class CRM centers to tell us what they do to make their service so unique. After studying as many as fifty such top performing centers we isolated ten characteristics that they all had in common. A list of these characteristics with a brief explanation follows:

1. *Economic Segmentation of Customers*

   Economic segmentation means that a company knows the actual value of each customer in terms of both annual revenue and profit generated. With this value segmentation in place, customers can be routed in the CRM center and treated differently based on their value. A high-value customer, for instance, may be routed to a shorter queue, or maybe to no queue at all. Airlines are especially good at value-based segmentation with their "frequent flyer" programs. Why have a 100,000-mile passenger wait in the same telephone queue as the occasional traveler?

2. *Closed-loop Workflow Processes*

   Closed-loop workflow processes means that every customer contact has a pre-designed sequence of steps leading to full closure of the customer contact in one contact (also known as "first-time final calls"). At the same time, this same customer contact may initiate other process opportunities, such as automatically alerting marketing of a sales opportunity.

3. *Institutional Memory*

   Institutional memory means that every customer contact is logged, processed, tracked, and shared—and the information disseminated and acted upon immediately. In these companies, customer information is considered a corporate asset. A concerted effort exists to do "root cause" analysis of customer contact data to better understand the reason for the call, and how to handle the call more efficiently in the future, or possibly avoid the call altogether.

8

4. *Customer Collaboration*

   Customer collaboration means that processes can be customized for individual customers with a lot of "one-to-one" thinking and design. Typically, companies that do well on this characteristic have many options for customer self-service and self-help.

5. *Touchpoint Alignment*

   Touchpoint alignment means that customer contact channels (telephone, e-mail, Web chat, and the like) are integrated such that, if a customer e-mails you first, for example, and then calls, the e-mail record is instantly available to the CSR.

6. *"Once and Done" Customer Contacts*

   "Once and Done" (also known as "first-time final") means that a customer call is handled on the first contact without being transferred or called back. For most CRM centers, this is not easy to do in light of the fact that information is not always conveniently located for the knowledge worker on the front line.

7. *Real-time Information Management*

   Real-time information management means that customer data acquired during customer calls is quickly and efficiently converted to real-time business intelligence for call center managers, as well as for other "customer-facing" departmental managers such as sales and marketing.

8. *Strategic Customer Listening Points*

   Strategic customer listening points means that the company has located customer satisfaction "listening" points close to where the customer "touchpoints" are. For instance, if the customer calls, there is an IVR-handled customer satisfaction survey done immediately after the call, not through follow-up surveys done hours or days after the call.

9. *Balanced Customer Scorecard*

   A balanced customer scorecard means that customer satisfaction is measured, logged, processed, and acted upon by "balancing" the customer's needs for quality with the company's need to make a profit.

10. *Total Experience Management*

Total experience management means that the complete customer "life cycle" of a company's product has been observed and studied, and that customer needs are anticipated and acted upon.

Customer Care Center Strategy

It does not matter where you are on the road to CRM. The art to CRM excellence lies in the ability of the team to continually uncover opportunities for peak performance in the areas of people, process, and technology (see figure 1.5).

Uncovering Opportunities

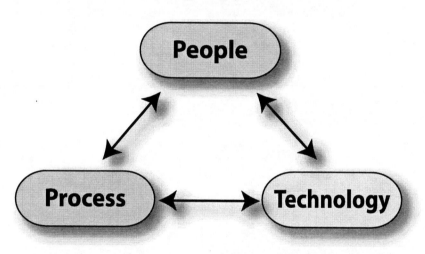

Figure 1.5. The key to CRM excellence is robust integration of people with processes and technology.

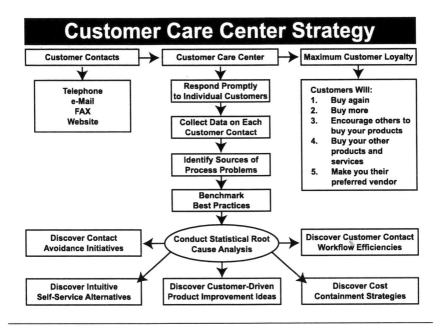

Figure 1.6. The strategy to create the ultimate customer experience

CRM Stakeholders

In figure 1.5 we saw people listed as a key to CRM. Let's start first with the people who have the most to gain or lose by a CRM implementation. We are calling them stakeholders. Stakeholders can include employees, executives, managers, customers, or vendors. They are anyone, no matter their level in an organization, who has the ability to influence the successful implementation and the use of CRM systems.

Stakeholders form the framework of relationships that surround any change effort and are the keys to the acceptance and support needed to get through an implementation. If the human aspect of the stakeholders is not dealt with from the very beginning of the project, studies show that the benefits of the program are not fully realized— implementation is delayed and higher costs result. This risk can be mitigated through a series of change management steps.

As leaders of CRM implementation, you need to do everything you can to get the support of stakeholders. You want to include several call center agents. Oftentimes the lack of full implementation is because the agents were not involved in choosing the new system and they don't use it. Then it comes down to $12/hr agents being in control of whether or not your $5 million CRM expenditure works.

Stakeholders (people) are the keys to the resources and the energy needed to overcome resistance and experiences associated with past change efforts. On average, 20% of people are natural supporters. The other 80% generally have some resistance or may be cynical, fearful, or even angry that this project is getting support while an initiative they were associated with earlier did not. In other cases they might have fears about:

- being outsourced themselves

- losing control of their department

- having their mistakes or decisions held up to criticism in the process of mapping out how business is currently done

- having an ongoing, internal, critical dialogue with themselves

- being criticized by a boss who sees mistakes as failure versus the opportunity to learn and grow.

The list of fears can go on and on. And sometimes bosses think that criticism will motivate someone to do a better job. Sometimes it might, but studies show that this drives very few work styles. The bottom line is, when employees don't get their work done, the business is losing money.

When planning and implementing CRM, there are people involved. Some of the people are your employees who will be doing the planning and implementing. Some of the people are the ones who will be using the CRM center: the customers. Understanding the impact of change on these two groups is important. The following list describes some of the changes a CRM implementation can bring:

1. Installing CRM or improving part of an existing CRM practice means that you are going to do business differently.

2. Doing business differently means you've changed the jobs of the people who do the work, from executives to managers to call center agents.

3. Changing their jobs means they will need to not only accept the change, but also get the training and skills to be able to do the job in the new way or they won't be able to follow the new process or use the new computer system.

4. Once you have established a new way for your employees to provide customer service to your customers, you must communicate that to the customers who need to use the new system—then monitor their reaction, incorporate their feedback, and gradually make more changes to the technology, process, or people part of the business.

The truth is, no matter what any vendor might intimate, technology systems are not turnkey operations. Part of that is because most technology must be integrated with legacy databases or computer systems, and people have to be trained in the new workflow. It is never as simple as buying a black box and being able to turn the key and have really happy, satisfied customers.

Your roadmap to CRM? It's contained in this book. Chapter 2 provides you with a structure to evaluate your CRM strategy and determine if that will accomplish your business objectives. Chapter 3 will explore the affect that changing how service is provided affects the whole CRM team and project risks like scope, timeline and budget. In chapter 4 we'll visit the issue of accessibility via business process mapping. And probably the most difficult aspect of CRM—is covered in chapter 5 on technology. We provide a strategy to determine how to choose technology. Chapter 6 is on Analytical CRM were we cover how to use the data collected on customers. Chapter 7 provides detail on customer satisfaction surveying and chapter 8 outlines a seven-step ROI process. We end with chapter 9 on benchmarking so that at end of day one truly knows what good enough is to create delighted customers in your industry.

Customer Obsession Graffiti #1

We saw an immediate improvement in call handling times. Little training was needed for the agents but the solution has made such a difference." "We are delighted with the results that computer telephony has brought to us."
—*Pam Young, Call Centre Manager BT (Sheffield)*

Customer Obsession Graffiti #2

For many customers, shopping on the Internet offers range, immediacy, discounts and flexibility. For others it offers frustration, non-deliveries, and unanswered questions. Customer service—or the lack of it—threatens this retail revolution. Recent research has shown that 66% of all those who visit an online store leave empty handed. As HelpMagic's Technical Director John Mears said, "There are some wonderful Web sites out there and there are people who want to use them, but may have questions that need to be answered. HelpMagic is the link between the two."

As Richard Patterson, HelpMagic's Managing Director said, "There are two types of Internet stores: those with customers service and those that won't succeed."

HelpMagic needed an interaction management solution to bring its customer service support online, and wanted a solutions provider who matched its innovative stance and shared the company vision. HelpMagic also needed the provider to implement quickly in order to run trials prior to its upcoming launch date. "It was a tall order, but we needed that kind of company if we were to succeed," said Patterson.

Visitors to HelpMagic clients' Web sites can now access information via a number of channels:

- e-mail a question
- enter into a real-time person-to-person text 'chat'
- request a call from an agent to discuss a question or problem over the telephone
- speak directly via voice links through the PC as they surf the Internet
- synchronize Web browsers and have the agent become a live shopping guide and direct them through the Web site.

—*John Mears, HelpMagic's Technical Director*

CHAPTER 2: CRM AS A CORPORATE STRATEGY

CRM Spending versus Business Results

Customer satisfaction is not a new concept. In fact it is as old as the days of bartering and trade. People would trade with others if they felt satisfied with what they were getting. Today the trade is between products and services and a customer's money, but the need to feel satisfied has never been greater. That feeling, "the customer experience," is the driving force. The difference between the bartering days of old and today's experience is that we rely heavily on technology to enable the relationship between the customer and the supplier. The question that seems to remain unanswered is: How best can we accomplish this satisfied feeling via technology, and is it, in fact, possible to do?

What we do know is that life is definitely different after CRM. It requires the transformation from being "company-centric" to being "customer-centric." This requires that everyone in the company adopt a "new attitude." It is not just about the call center agents; everyone—from engineering to accounting—must think in terms of *reporting directly to the customer*. Think about that for a moment. If someone in accounting had to answer to the customer, would they do their job differently? One great example of occurred at a company where 9% of the calls were of the "when is my bill due" variety. When we looked at the bills that were generated by accounting, we found that there was a date on them, but the date was the day the bill was printed, not the date the bill was due! We went to accounting and asked them to add a line to the bill stating when it was due. Accounting started thinking about the customer and whether what they were doing was really serving the customer or not. They made the change.

In addition to individual departments transforming to customer-centricity, the whole company can no longer work as independent silos. The mindset that engineering has little or nothing to do with marketing no longer applies. After CRM every department is dependent on each other to create the end result: a satisfied customer. The burning question: *How to change the company so that the leadership and the employee are "obsessed" with serving the customer?* In this chapter we focus on the leadership strategy to accomplish customer obsession. Without customer obsession as the underlying driver, CRM could be another technology disappointment.

> - 69.3% of CRM installations failed to meet all goals.
> - 45.3% were late.
> - 36.8% were over budget.
> - 31.7% did not produce meaningful results.
>   —Selling Power, CSO Forum

With a large number of CRM projects not meeting their objectives, we started to ask:

- What percentage of these companies' executives were "obsessed" with satisfying the customer?
- What kinds of technology are being purchased?
- Has the company transformed from being company-centric to customer-centric?
- Does top management support the change in corporate mindset to customer-centricity?
- Have all the employees, not just the call center agents, changed their behavior to reflect customer-centricity?
- Did the team map out all the processes that contribute to customer service?
- Did they reengineer any of the processes to make them more efficient and effective?
- What priority, if at all, was training given?
- Did the CRM have support (apply money, capital and people) to adequately implement the project or was it done on a shoestring with people having to do their regular jobs plus the CRM implementation?
- Did they consider an ASP or outsourcing model for agents and/or the infrastructure or did they decide to do it all themselves?
- Does the CRM technology really enable a better customer relationship?
- What is the return on investment for the technology?

When CRM does not produce the results expected, what went wrong? Did the salespeople overpromise or might the company's expectations have been too high? Might it have something to do with how the change in providing customer service affected the people and organization who deliver it? Was the human element (the people providing the service) considered a strategic part of the technology implementation, or were the change management, training, communication plans, and the like still being cut out of large technology budgets as a cost-savings measure? Did the company look at their business processes? Did they not consider this part of a technology purchase?

In the midst of the CRM and technology chaos, we felt the need to write a book about how to succeed when implementing CRM technology. The goal of this chapter is to help you with your strategy. We will look at ways to connect customer satisfaction and technology with an outcome that enables not only a great CRM implementation, but enhanced customer satisfaction. In order for CRM to be successful, both the customer and supplier of goods and services need to feel so good about the interaction that they continue to want to buy from each other for a lifetime. This is what we mean by an excellent "customer obsession."

So in this chapter you can look forward to many things that will help you in your journey towards a successful CRM implementation. These include a recap of CRM history so that we can see where we started and where we are going. Then we will introduce you to strategizing about customer obsession by using our Magic Squares. These Magic Squares are a proven road map for CRM strategy. We will also explore the importance of leadership in CRM, and CRM as a corporate differentiator.

CRM History

In today's fast-moving and highly competitive marketplace, products come and products go. For companies large and small, the most important real asset, with measurable long-term value, is loyal, one-to-one customer relationships.

The concept of a customer relationship is not new at all. The focus on proactively "managing" many customer relationships individually is very new. Customer relationship management (CRM) as we know it today began in the early 1990s when several technologies evolved into "prime time" almost simultaneously. These technology enhancements included all of the following:

1. computing power became ubiquitous, i.e., everyone had computing power,

2. computing devices spanned the complete spectrum from mainframes to hand-held PCs,

3. the proliferation of "everybody is on-line," placed enormous "access" capabilities in the hands of "front line" customer service professionals, all the way from telephone agents to even the feet-on-the-street sales professionals—the many parts of customer service "got connected."

4. through the Internet, access to information by the public became almost like an electric utility,

5. data storage and retrieval devices got smaller, more compact, and very inexpensive,

6. wireless communications grew exponentially, namely, cell phones, pagers, PDA, and the like,

7. database warehousing capabilities improved substantially,

8. and finally, tools for data-mining, also known as data analytics, became very user-friendly, intuitive, and real time.

All of the above "happenings" in technology made it possible for us finally to know a lot about each individual customer, and to have this information accessible in "real time." Because of the availability of customer data, this data could be quickly processed into useful business intelligence to actually guide decisions about how to manage a customer relationship on a one-to-one basis—incredible progress—that was not possible until the CRM revolution began.

With global competition, many products had been reduced to mere commodities that were difficult to differentiate through features, functions, quality, or price—in fact, great value, great quality, and great prices became the "table stakes" of doing business in the new millennium. The paradigm shift was definitely toward customer service as a differentiator. In particular, the new focus was on CRM solutions through which we could give customers easy access to mission-critical information about products and service. The trend in CRM has logically fueled the growing importance of the multi-channel customer "answer" center of today.

With the emergence of e-business, customers can contact companies through many channels including the telephone, e-mail, Web site, chat, VOIP, kiosk, FAX, wireless, and many more. Through these electronic "touchpoints," customers are selecting products based on a new feature, namely, the ease of "accessibility" to information before, during, and after a purchase.

Because of this new focus on accessibility, executives now recognize the CRM as a significant revenue generator, perhaps the surest investment they can make in getting new customers, retaining existing customers, enhancing customer value, and ultimately improving their bottom-line profits.

With the new-found strategic importance of the "CRM" center, a vast array of emerging technology solutions began to surface to enable better customer relationships. In figure 2.1, we highlight the critical components of a robust and successful CRM deployment.

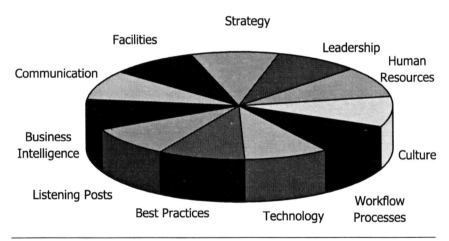

Figure 2.1. The various service imperatives for successful CRM

For businesses in the 1980s, technology became focused on automation for efficiency. Financial reporting systems became very popular. CRM as we know it today did not really start until the early 1990s. At that time, it was a computerized system used to understand customer profiles and buying patterns. A lot of stock was put into marketing and looking for trends, but a systematic way of recording the customer experience was waiting to be born. So CRM began as a *product* to help companies determine the "what" and "how many" that were ordered by customers—in other words, market research and account management.

In the early 1990s, CRM was more focused on providing customer information rather than a strategy to manage the relationship with the customer. This was because in the early 1990s the focus was on providing *efficiencies*. Today, the driver is to become more *effective* at customer relationship management. Hopefully, this distinction can help to clarify the change in strategies that are required for CRM today. Yesterday CRM meant a product. Today it means a system (people, processes, and technology) to get, and grow customers who remain loyal forever.

To better understand the evolution from product to system of CRM, let's see what was going on. In the midst of the development of CRM information systems along came Y2K. With the advent and scare of the Y2K issues, attention was quickly diverted to choosing a solution to what was deemed by many to be the downfall of computers, as we knew them. Companies began focusing on their information system's data storage, and in particular, dates. At about the same time, the big consulting firms saw a market for helping companies get more organized, and they were looking for ways to be more organization-centric. By focus alone, information systems (IS) are very different than customer-centric-CRM systems. This "organizational information system" evolved as a product or solution called Enterprise Resource Planning (ERP).

The Y2K problem gave companies a reason to reorganize their IT and added popular ERP solutions. It was only natural that when CRM began, it also followed in the footsteps of ERP and Y2K and was thought of by many as a product. What the business community discovered along the way was that CRM is far more than just a product. Instead, in order to really serve the customer, CRM means much more. It means not only a technology solution, but a complete transformation from *organization-centricity* to the new thought paradigm of *customer-centricity*. Technology would be part of CRM, but CRM would also entail the synergy of people and processes to accomplish the goal of customer-centricity.

> We tend to meet any new situation by reorganizing. And what a wonderful method reorganizing is for creating the illusion of progress while producing inefficiency and demoralization.
> —Petronium, Greek Philosopher, 210 B.C.

The quote above is one of our favorites because many times we decide to take on a CRM implementation to "organize how we deal with the customer," but without a CRM strategy, we can end up creating inefficiency and demoralization of the workforce.

Dataquest reports that the worldwide CRM service market generated over $19.9 billion in revenue in 2000, a 28% increase from 1999 (Spiegel, 2001). The average budget for end-users CRM is currently over $1 million per company. This spending is expected to double over the next 12 months, and Gartner Group is predicting that CRM investments will reach $125 billion in 2005 (Mello, 2002). Says Kevin Scott, marketing analyst at AMR Research, "This rise in expenditures is not surprising, given that top management is buying deeply into CRM right now. With the downturn in the economy, they are turning to see how they can make marketing more efficient, how they can retain customers, and how they can get more revenue from existing customers" (Spiegel, 2001).

CRM = being so obsessed with your customer's satisfaction that you change the way you do business

How well do you know your customers? Do you know their preferences to buy, much less what it would take to up-sell or cross-sell them? Let's look at a story about Intel. This narrative demonstrates one company's drive to not only re-think their strategy, but actually change the way they do business. For CRM to be successful, you will most likely need to change how you are doing business. This means it cannot be just boxes that get checked off on an executive's to-do list—it means that organizational transformation on all levels must take place.

WHO are my REAL customers? The story of the 386 processor is one of our favorites for two reasons. One, it helps us to think outside our normal thoughts to see an example of how someone redefined their customer base and saved a product line from disaster. Secondly, it is a true example where a company not only thought about things differently, but also allocated the money, people, resources, time, and

21

commitment to make it happen. It was not just some management initiative *de jour*. It actually happened.

Here is what happened at Intel. The chip manufacturer had created a faster, more powerful computer-processing chip, the 386. In doing so, they thought they had the market cornered. Everyone would be buying the chip. To their complete surprise, they found that the computer manufacturers were not responding. When Intel's marketing people went to find out why, the computer manufacturer said there wasn't any market interest, the 286 processor was fine. "But how could that be," Intel asked, "this is the next best thing to apple pie!" Then Intel's management went to the computer stores and asked why the storeowners had not been ordering computers with this new chip. Again, a similar answer—there was no customer interest.

Puzzled and frustrated, a multi-disciplinary team of marketing, business development, and engineering-types gathered to figure out this conundrum. They went directly to the people who buy computers in the computer stores. They asked PC consumers if they would like a computer that could run larger applications—applications that would let them do graphic design or make movies. "Well, of course, that would be great!" they responded. "Where can I get such a computer?"

This is when the light bulb went on. *Intel had been marketing to the wrong customer*. The real customer in this case was the computer user, not the PC manufacturer, and not the computer store owner. And hence was born the brilliant marketing campaign of *Intel Inside*, complete with a jingle, so that every time a computer user started up their computer, they would be reminded of the smart choice they had made in purchasing the computer. They had "Intel Inside," and that meant they could go as fast as any personal computer in the world! A great buyer experience was rekindled with every logon.

Ask yourself the following questions: Who are my customers? Who do I think my customers are? Who are my competitor's customers? Why do they buy the other guy's products over mine?

We wanted to use this story of the chip manufacturer who began selling directly to the PC users to recoin the term CRM. We want to emphasize the idea of **Customer Relationship Management**. CRM means understanding who your REAL customers are and managing that relationship as well as Intel did. In addition, you want to determine how easy it is for that customer to get your products and services. Do they even know your product exists? The PC buyer did not even know about the Intel chip. The ease with which customers can obtain information is what we call accessibility. Excellent accessibility means that no matter how a customer tries to get in touch with you, it is easy and rewarding. In other words, they are satisfied with the interaction or experience. We will cover accessibility again in chapter 4 when we look at business process design.

The take-away from this example is that Intel rearranged its sales channels to reach the end-user. How did they do this? By changing their strategy! If companies want CRM to work, they have to understand who their customers are and what their needs are. This requires business rules and mapping out the business processes and redesigning them so that you are reaching your REAL customer. And all of that requires a CRM strategy.

Who is the customer? Is your CRM system really serving the consumer of your product?

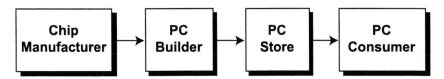

Upgrade 286 processor to 386 processor.
No sales via this sales process.

Figure 2.2. Intel's experience with its "real customer"

Introduction to Our Magic Squares

In order to avoid repeating history, we need to learn from it. While working at Oracle, Ad Nederlof created a format to help his customers think about their strategy when buying technology. Now we use it in describing a strategy for CRM. Figure 2.3a is a set of squares that we call our "Magic Squares." The magic part is that if they are followed, the results of the technology can be amazing. If one does not use a system to prioritize tasks and steps, then you will most likely find yourself in the same boat as most technology buyers—overspent and underutilized.

Who's in Charge	Action to Take	Business Process/Training /Change Management	Information System Requirements	Hardware and Infra-structure Requirements
CEO	Plan	1	2	3
CIO/CFO	Deploy/Build	4	5	6
COO/CIO	Maintain	7	8	9

Figure 2.3a. Our Magic Squares for strategic CRM implementation

On the left side of our Magic Squares (figure 2.3a) is a list of the point person in each area. In general it is the CEO, CIO, and the COO along with the CFO. The next column designates three main actions for each of them to take:

- plan
- build and deploy
- maintain.

Across the top of figure 2.3a are the various parts of the implementation process:

- change management, business process mapping, reengineering, training—essentially, the people management
- information system requirements
- hardware and infrastructure requirements.

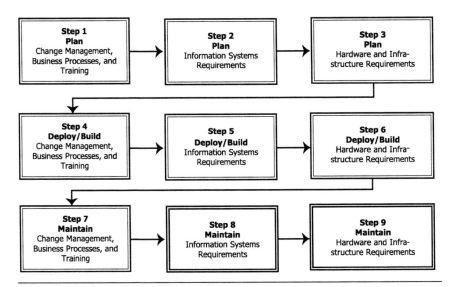

Figure 2.3b. The flow diagram of our Magic Squares

The way to use our magic squares is shown in figure 2.3b. You start in square number 1. When you have finished the actions required to complete that square, you move to square 2, then to 3, and so on. Let's take a look at what each step entails:

Square 1 - Plan the Change Management, Business Processes and Training

In this box is the planning for change management, business processes, and training of the people. This is the organizational development aspect of the CRM project. It is the job of the CEO to take his or her three-year plan and communicate that to the CIO so that he or she can create a team to outline the business processes that affect customer service and product delivery. An expert in change management will guide the team to create a communication plan that tells everyone what is happening in the company as well as guides the company through the changes that will be happening throughout the life cycle of the CRM project.

Square 2 - Plan the Information Systems Requirements

This is the square where the CEO tells the CIO the business objectives of the CRM system, and the CIO recommends the types of solutions that could deliver the functionality requested by the business objective via the business processes and business rules.

25

The decision to use an ASP or outsourcing model for some or all of the components in the system has to be made here.

Square 3 - Plan the Infrastructure Requirements

In this square, the CIO recommends the types of hardware that would allow the software to operate to accomplish the business objectives. Discussions about legacy systems are started here—to plan for the changes that will need to be made when integrating them later. The decision to potentially gut the whole legacy system and start from scratch needs to be made here. The decision to use an ASP or outsourcing model for some or all of the components in the system has to be made here.

Square 4 - Build and Deploy the Business Processes and Training

This is the square where the CIO works with the CFO to create a budget to do the work required to purchase the software and hardware. The issues of reengineering the process are very important for effectiveness and efficiency. In addition, the plans for integration begin here. The COO works with various divisions to map out all the new workflow processes and update them before the CIO buys hardware and software.

Square 5 - Build and Deploy the Information Systems Requirements

The CIO and COO work with various divisions to build and deploy the software. This can include workflow management, CTI, and more. One of the most important aspects of CRM is integrating all the other technology initiatives with the customer strategy. This would include ERP, supply chain, shared services, HR applications, and so on. The integration of all of these technology systems is the reason why square 5 is so difficult if not planned for in square 2.

Square 6 - Build and Deploy the Infrastructure Requirements

In this square, the CIO and COO work with various divisions to build and deploy the hardware. This can include open frameworks with computers, networks, switches, databases, ACDs, IVRs, desktop software, and more.

Square 7 - Maintain the Business Processes and Training

In this square, the CIO works with the COO to maintain and update the business processes and rules as well as to continue to train people.

Square 8 - Maintain the Information Systems Requirements

In this square, the COO works with various divisions to maintain the CRM system. How maintenance is carried out depends on what model the team has chosen—ASP, outsourcing, or whether they kept everything internal to their company.

Square 9 - Maintain the Infrastructure Requirements

In this square, the COO works with various divisions to maintain the CRM infrastructure. Again, here the maintenance depends on whether they used an ASP, outsourcing, or in-house model.

What is the problem with most technology implementations? Leaders think they are looking for a CRM product or solution, so they start at squares 5 and 6. Without the completion of squares 1 to 4, no CEO should allocate any money to the CRM project. It is certain failure. While following our Magic Squares is a new paradigm in technology project implementation, it is a necessary change in thought leadership.

Five years ago the CEO would say we need a certain type of technology and the CIO would start at squares 5 and 6. Even before that, in the 1980s, many times technology companies would build the hardware (square 6) and then figure out an application that could run on top of it (square 5), and then figure out how people could use that application (square 4). This is traditionally how advances in technology have taken place. However, *the progression to develop technology advances are different than those that one should take when looking at a technology project to solve a business issue.* The problem is that this distinction is not commonly known or followed in practice. This is because the CEO oftentimes is not versed in technology and hands the decision to the CIO. The CIO, who was schooled in the traditional implementation development of technology (starting with squares 6, 5, and then 4) doesn't even think about starting with square 1. And it is no wonder why the reason business process rules and design are often skipped. If the CIO is the type of manager in the old days, i.e., an EDP manager, then they might not even think of looking at the planning steps 1-3. In fact, our research

27

shows that nearly 70% of the technology budgets are spent on maintenance, 25% on build/deploy and 5% on planning.

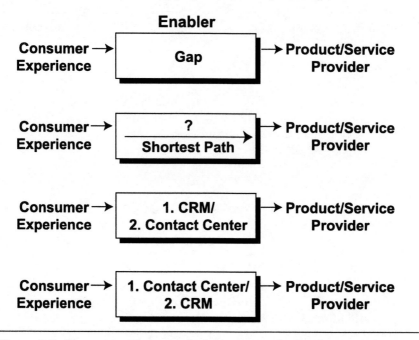

Figure 2.4. Shortest path to reach the customer is via the contact center

Keep It Super Simple (KISS)

Rather than trying to automate everything in a company's interaction with a customer, we feel that it is important to start simple. This is shown in figure 2.4. A consumer wants a product. What's the shortest path to enable them? When CRM began, everyone felt they had to start with CRM in the call center. We know in fact that many executives already think the call center is a strategic part of the company's business strategy (figure 2.5). So if the call center is already a mission critical center, then why not launch the CRM project there?

What if the CRM project manager started with the call center and then expanded the CRM project from there? This is the strategy we suggest. It is doable and great results are possible.

What is the relative importance of the call center in your company's business strategy?

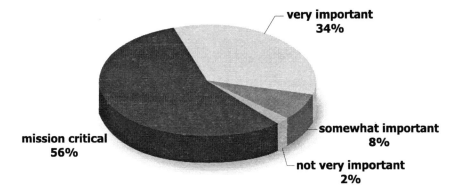

Source: Purdue University Research (mini survey 2-1)

Figure 2.5. Our research shows that executives feel the call center is mission critical.

When companies attack the CRM *call to action*, they tend to, in their hurry, bite off the whole "enchilada," when one bite at a time would be far more manageable. The point here, with respect to strategy, is to segment the implementation into pieces. Start with the call center, add the contact center components, and then add sales automation, marketing, and then move into integration with ERP, HR, supply chain, etc. In the end, the shortest path to customer satisfaction is excellent channel integration at the contact center via routing technology with analytical capabilities to feed customer requirements into the business to improve it.

Part of implementing this new strategy for CRM is building a CRM center that enables the agent to serve the customer properly. This comes from changing the call center strategy from a back-office cost center to a front-line ambassadorship. It means hiring the right people, paying them well, training and coaching them, and rewarding them well. It means enabling them with technology that has instant customer identification, records, channel integration, etc. We will explore ways to accomplish these goals in other chapters. For now, let's look at the people strategy for CRM; in particular, what is required at the leadership level.

29

CRM Begins With the Top Management

People-Skills Requirements

Figure 2.1 shows the range of service imperatives required for CRM to be successful. From this diagram we can see that there is far more to CRM than just a software application or some hardware. Along with the changes in technology strategy, there is also a need for new skill-sets in the executive branches. The CEO needs to understand technology, and the CIO needs to understand the business objectives the technology should accomplish. Then the CIO needs to determine how the software and hardware will accomplish these business objectives. Executives can no longer hand off these responsibilities, but rather, they must act as a finely tuned team. An analogy is the difference between eating a chocolate chip cookie and knowing how to bake good ones yourself. In other words, a CEO can't just know about great chocolate chip cookies, he or she must be well versed in what goes into making a great cookie!

The CEO can use our Magic Squares to talk to the leaders of each square. It is imperative that the team members also work strategically and tactically together with a diagram like this. And the CEO must be interested in all the boxes and oversee them all for success. Companies that don't invest in squares 1 to 4, are setting themselves up for failure in squares 5 and 6.

The CIO today needs to have a full range of technology knowledge. But in addition to being on top of the latest developments in technology, the CIO must be fully versed in change management, business process mapping, reengineering, strategic thinking, and planning to be able to select technology that translates into making the business run smoothly and profitably. They also need people skills, as they will have to lead a multidisciplinary team. *Today information technology (IT) is a people business.*

As a leader you will also need the best project managers you can find. This is an area where you do not want to skimp on qualifications, salary, or experience. Project managers must have people and change management skills. They must be able to motivate people, convince them, be a great speaker, and handle stress as well as all the other HR issues that are required in handling people and teams. They also need to be able to communicate with vendors.

Managing Expectations

To succeed in a technology implementation, it pays to heed a rule of thumb called "Dr. Hans Leenaars, Professor at Amsterdam University, Expectation Filter." When implementing CRM to manage the expectation of the team:

- Take the cost and multiply it by 2.
- Take the time and multiply it by 2.
- Take the performance and divide it by 2.

If you use this expectation filter, then you should be pretty close to your target. The reason it is so difficult to hit the target right on is that the expectations in a CRM project are not managed well. The fact is that the vendor wants the order and the CEO wants a solution. This makes for a dangerous combination. Why? Because companies are so demanding in their expectations in the sales process that the vendors, under pressure to get the sale, oftentimes say yes because they are backed into a corner. You rarely hear a good sales person come back to their sales manager and say, "I was very honest with the CEO, but I lost the deal." Many sales professionals oversell the capabilities or underestimate the time requirements.

As a leader you can also save a lot of money by doing things right the first time. Correcting things or doing rework costs more. It is better to know the project is really going to take two years than to think it will take one year and experience two years of frustration.

Decreasing the Failure Rate

Here are some tips for decreasing the CRM failure rate:

- Don't change the standard solution offered by the vendor. Each change means a change in every square. It is better to change the organization to meet the technology solution. You must train people to work with the new system—otherwise they won't use it, and then, what is the point of installing it if no one is really using it?

- Don't buy more functionality than you need. If you did the business process mapping, you will know what functionality you need. Our favorite saying on this is, "Don't go for the sheep with five legs." In other words, yes, the sheep with five legs is really fascinating, but does a sheep need five legs to stand? Stop yourself from asking the impossible, when the impossible is not needed to accomplish the business goal.

The more you tailor a solution, the more risk you will encounter in time, budget, and scope. As a "rule of thumb," if the design, implementation, and integration cost five times the license fee, then you are changing the solution too much. This is because change also means more maintenance costs down the road. If possible, it should only be less than two times the cost.

The role of the systems integrator is extremely important in steps 1-3. In fact, there might be several different experts that guide the planning, for instance, an organizational development person might focus on step 1, where someone with a background in software might lead the plan in step 2, and so on. When choosing an integrator, be careful that they don't just focus on step 5 versus 1, 2, 3, and 4. The big bucks are in step 5 for them, but the key to success for you is in steps 1-4.

Loyalty-based CRM Management

Loyalty-based management is about your people: your customers, employees, and investors. Loyalty is based on motivation and behavior, not on marketing, finance, or product development. At companies where loyalty-based leadership is predominant, employees are proud that they treat their customers and each other the way they would want to be treated. Their work experience is balanced between their own goals and the organization's dedication to serving the customer. Work that sacrifices personal principles drains employees' energy. When work is congruent with personal principles, it is a source of energy, and pride results. Pride is therefore a powerful source of motivation and energy.

Pride doubles the economic advantage inherent in a loyalty-based CRM solution. In chapter 3 we'll explore the people challenges—the part that connects employees' goals to the customer service goals so that both the company and the employees are served. Employees' jobs can become congruent with personal principles and work can be a source of energy that transforms service providers into loyalty-based employees. Pride also can help transform managers into loyalty-based managers and executives. But first, let's look at a quick example of the economics of pride to further convince you of the value of people.

An example of a company that knows the economic value of loyalty-based management is USAA, the San Antonio insurance and investment management firm that serves active and retired military officers and their families. Under the leadership of CEO General Robert F. McDermott, who insists that, "Customers and employees are both precious resources," USAA grew from $207 million in assets to $34 billion in 26 years. Even with this hundredfold increase in assets, the company's employee base has expanded only by a factor of five. Employee attrition rates shrank from 43% to 5%. The customer retention is 99%. McDermott, with a background as a professional officer and educator, turned the theory of loyalty-based management into an applied science.

As a first step, the company changed its focus to "people first," then to process and technology. With the focus on people, they invested $130 million in technology to enhance service and loyalty to create measures to monitor progress in those areas. With a company focus on understanding the economics that underpin loyalty-based management, they built that understanding into all their decision-making processes. They refined their ability to learn from failure (from customer and employee attrition) and to achieve continuous measurable improvement in the creation and allocation of value.

Our book will review ideas and case studies for you to better understand your employee base so that you can get the return on your human capital asset, and transform your culture into a loyalty-based organization. Much of what we have found is based on how you communicate with each other. Without a method to understand how communication is currently done and where the gaps are, you can't begin to create this kind of culture. Why do we still think of things like employee loyalty or motivation as soft skills and not respect the effects they have on the bottom line?

CRM as a Corporate Differentiator

This book is dedicated to helping you to avoid falling into the financial and implementation gaps that happened in the ERP gold rush. We will try to raise questions and red flags and to give you the tools to understand what you are buying in the world of CRM, as well as to determine if CRM meets your business needs and objectives. To do that you must become obsessed with your customer, because CRM is one of the most difficult endeavors you will ever undertake. If you are not "customer obsessed," you'll give up long before achieving your business goals.

An example of customer loyalty economics is given below (Reichheld, 1996).

If a credit card company can increase its retention of customers by 5% each year, then total lifetime profits from a typical customer will rise an average of 75%. This retention translates into a company's growth potential. Let's see how: If Company 1 has a customer retention rate of 95% and Company 2 has a customer retention rate of 90%, the company's growth rates are sizable different:

- Company 1: 5% loss of profit per year
- Company 2: 10% loss of profit per year.

If both companies acquire new customers at the rate of 10% per year, Company 1 will have a 5% net growth in customer inventory per year, while Company 2 will have none. Over fourteen years, Company 1 will double in size and Company 2 will have no real growth at all. And other things being equal, a 5-percentage-point-advantage in customer retention translates into a growth advantage equal to doubling of customer inventory every 14 years. An advantage of 10 percentage points accelerates the doubling to seven years. In order to accomplish these kinds of bottom-line effects, the leadership strategy must focus on how to create loyalty among its customers, which also means retention of its employees who serve those customers. And research has shown that customers will react very differently, depending on which of the three states of mind they are in at the time (Anton, 1991): those who are dissatisfied, those who are satisfied, and those who are delighted. These differences show up in the following actions:

- willingness to recommend
- intention to repurchase
- positive word of mouth.

So in this chapter we have covered CRM history, a new strategy to implement CRM as well as the requirements of leadership to make CRM a corporate differentiator. In the next chapter we will explore how leaders can more effectively deal with how employees feel about the changes technology will bring to their jobs. When leaders understand change, they are more able to manage the human capital asset so necessary to CRM implementation. Let's take a look at the human aspect to CRM...

Customer Obsession Graffiti #3

"Whatever information we have about that customer comes up on their screen pop. When you multiply seconds on a phone call by millions of phone calls, it means substantial savings to the organization."
—*Cloene Goldsborough-Davis, VP, Sprint PCS*

Customer Obsession Graffiti #4

Barclays identified the need to develop its existing call distribution system into a business-based technology solution that could handle large volumes of phone calls and future e-mail and Web-based interactions, while delivering high levels of service to its customers.

To improve overall efficiency, Barclays also wanted to boost the functionality of its Interactive Voice Response System (IVR) units, and to better utilize the information stored in the bank's customers information system, by providing sales and service advisors with each customer's bank account history during every query or transaction.

"We evaluated various solutions in the computer telephony integration (CTI) market," explains David Craggs, head of Contact Centers at Barclays.

Paul Pugal, head of operations at Barclays Contact Centers, says, "The ability to link voice and data and to keep these attached at stages of the call cycle's life was key to us. Advisors are more efficient in handling a customer's query thanks to the data received in the screen pop and it is easier to engage in conversation with customers because they do not have to re-key account numbers or ask for information twice."
—*David Craggs, Manager, Barclays Bank Contact Centers*

The People Part of "People, Process and CRM Technology"

In the previous chapter we looked at the importance of a solid business strategy to ensure the success of customer relationship management. However, the best business strategy is only as successful as the people who execute it. Motivated, excited employees, who are willing to go the distance, are essential to carrying out the multitude of steps in a CRM implementation. With the new emphasis on CRM, not only do we find that the people are now playing a larger role, but we also find that there is a new demand for "people-culture" change, including faster communications, more detailed and timely information about customers, and more precise measurements of cost and quality to provide excellence. As business is accelerating at the speed of the Internet, employees are being asked to do more than they ever have done before. These rapidly expanding demands are driving the force to re-consider the coordinates of people, process, and technology (see figure 3.1).

Here are six mistakes companies make when applying CRM:

1. Believe vendor hype and unrealistic expectations
2. No customer strategy
3. Poor preparation for change
4. Absence of executive leadership
5. Neglecting metrics
6. Forgetting that "C" stands for "customer".

In the past, the people part of a technology implementation was not given much thought. Change management, the process to manage the people part, has not been widely accepted as a critical success factor. In fact, when management looks to cut an implementation budget, change management and training are the first to go. However, our research and experience shows that, to maximize the ROI for implementing the state-of-the-art CRM solutions, managing change and preparing people is a top priority.

PEOPLE, PROCESS, AND TECHNOLOGY

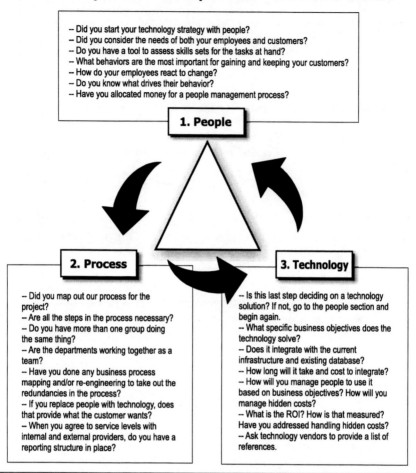

-- Did you start your technology strategy with people?
-- Did you consider the needs of both your employees and customers?
-- Do you have a tool to assess skills sets for the tasks at hand?
-- What behaviors are the most important for gaining and keeping your customers?
-- How do your employees react to change?
-- Do you know what drives their behavior?
-- Have you allocated money for a people management process?

1. People

2. Process

-- Did you map out our process for the project?
-- Are all the steps in the process necessary?
-- Do you have more than one group doing the same thing?
-- Are the departments working together as a team?
-- Have you done any business process mapping and/or re-engineering to take out the redundancies in the process?
-- If you replace people with technology, does that provide what the customer wants?
-- When you agree to service levels with internal and external providers, do you have a reporting structure in place?

3. Technology

-- Is this last step deciding on a technology solution? If not, go to the people section and begin again.
-- What specific business objectives does the technology solve?
-- Does it integrate with the current infrastructure and existing database?
-- How long will it take and cost to integrate?
-- How will you manage people to use it based on business objectives? How will you manage hidden costs?
-- What is the ROI? How is that measured? Have you addressed handling hidden costs?
-- Ask technology vendors to provide a list of references.

Figure 3.1. People, Process and Technology Triad

Because of the importance of people to a CRM project, we wanted to devote a whole chapter to the impact people have on the implementation of CRM technology. In this chapter we will review data from our Purdue University research that shows the critical role employees play in delivering customer service. We do, however, want to emphasize here that it is not just the agents who are important to the success of a CRM project, but that it is every employee in the corporation. It includes the technology team, the people in marketing, business development, product engineering, and manufacturing. Every single person plays a very important role in making the customer happy.

When CRM technology is implemented, nearly everyone's job changes. The processes change, the computer system changes, and as a result the people have to adjust to a new way of thinking and doing things in order to serve the customer. In many corporations, just the transition from a company-centric culture to a customer-centric culture can provide interesting challenges. Because we have found the people to be such an underlying factor in successfully delivering a well-integrated system, in this chapter we will explore the science of change and its affect on people in a CRM project.

Why Have a Change Management Process?

One of the symptoms most often observed when the people part of implementations is not done well is that people don't really use the new CRM technology. In fact, we see more and more companies getting caught up in buying the best technology available, only to find later that all the "bells and whistles" are not being used, let alone the basic functionality. We have also found that the maximum ROI occurs when a comprehensive people change management program, that includes every employee–from the front line agents to the CEO– guides the CRM implementation in the company.

The reason for a comprehensive change management program is that CRM really is all about change. For example, when a company decides that they want to either add a CRM program to their existing customer service strategy or upgrade their existing CRM practice, what they are really saying is that they want to *change the way they are providing service*. There is the "as is" state of the customer service, and there is the "could be" state after the technology is implemented. The need to go from the "as is" to the "could be" state means that there is a gap. To close that gap requires that things change. The operative word that we want to emphasize here is **change**.

> "If the word excellence is to be applicable in the future, it requires a redefinition. Excellent companies don't believe in excellence—only in constant change. Excellent companies will know how to cherish chaos and thrive on change."
> —Tom Peters, *Thriving on Chaos*

We find that what goes unaddressed or underestimated in many CRM implementations is the effect that change has on people, in other words, the human capital asset. The simple fact is that when the way the service is provided changes, it means employees also have to change what they were doing to provide service in the new way. In spite of this fact, what is practically ignored in many CRM project implementations is the fact that it is human nature to resist change. Humans resist any change, not just change concerning CRM technology. Humans resist change even when it is a good thing. It's the way we're wired. We will take a look later in this chapter at brain chemistry, and how change affects the brain and thus one's perspective on change. While the issues with changing technology, workflow, or processes are important to the success of a CRM implementation, nothing has more effect on the implementation than how the changes were accepted on the interpersonal level. In a recent CRM Forum survey conducted, 87% of the respondents listed change management problems as the primary case of failure for CRM projects. (Mello, 2002)

Data on the Importance of CRM Centers

We wanted to compare the demand on the agents in a CRM center to the amount of time, money, and focus is placed on training and developing these agents or giving them the tools they need to do their job during technology implementations. Our Purdue University research studies (figure 3.2) show that 55% of executives are committed to achieving customer service via the CRM center.

To create a successful CRM center, we believe that one must integrate the people with the process and technology in a systematized manner. Unfortunately what we see in companies is something other than that. While executives say they are committed to the CRM center success, we found that the attitudes of many executives about budgeting time and money to the human aspect ranged from denial to skepticism to downright indignation. Their attitude can be summed up by the statement of one executive who told us, "The people will do as they are told or we will find a replacement." We also found that leaders with those attitudes were the ones who are the most disappointed with the ROI results of their CRM implementations. Since dealing with change is the precursor that makes or breaks a CRM implementation, the correlations between the denial of the human element and the failure to deliver on the CRM initiative disappointment makes sense.

Let's now look at the data that show what is important to the call center manager and the agents in creating a successful CRM center. Figure 3.3 shows the biggest challenges facing a CRM center manager. The top six are all addressed by a comprehensive CRM solution set. In order to address these issues, CRM center managers said what they thought would help the center the most is shown in figure 3.4.

How personally committed are the senior executives in your company to achieving high service levels through the CRM center?

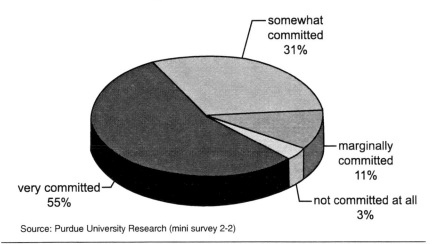

Source: Purdue University Research (mini survey 2-2)

Figure 3.2. Fifty-five percent of the executives are fully committed to achieving customer service via the CRM center.

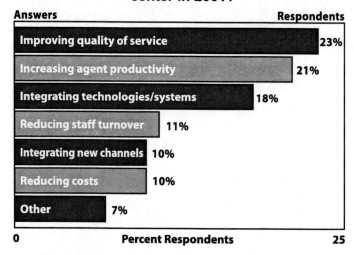

What are the biggest challenges facing your CRM center in 2001?

Source: Purdue University Research (published in *CCNews* Oct. 2001)

Figure 3.3. CRM center managers' responses to being asked: What are the biggest challenges facing your CRM center?

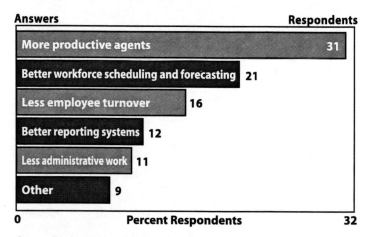

Which of the following do you think would help improve your contact center?

Source: Purdue University Research (published in *CCNews* Oct. 2001)

Figure 3.4. This survey shows what CRM center managers thought would help the center the most.

When asked how the challenges are going to be addressed, the CRM manager responded with:

- develop in-house processes (21%)
- improve employee performance (20%)
- increase employee coaching (19%)
- develop in-house solutions (16%)
- purchase new technology (14%)
- other (10%).

Of the people, process, and technology triad, 39% of the solution is related to the people, whereas technology is only 14%. The conclusion from the data is clear: CRM center managers understand the value of the human capital asset.

Customer Satisfaction versus Agent Performance

Now that we have established the CRM center manager's need for enhancing the human capital asset, let's look at how important agent performance is to customer satisfaction. Since our book is about customer obsession, we want to keep reminding the reader that the whole reason we care about agent and employee performance is that it has a direct correlation to customer satisfaction. If employee performance is a pivotal, mission-critical success criterion, then it must also become a daily "obsession" of the executives.

Figure 3.5a shows that the most important driver of customer satisfaction is the agent's ability to complete the call in one phone call. When a call is resolved on the first call, without any transfer or call-backs, it is known as a "first time final" call. When we looked at this data further, we found that there is an almost linear relationship between first/final calls and caller satisfaction (figure 3.4b). The conclusion? The strongest driving force for excellent customer service is the agent's performance. In other words, your CRM center is only as good as the agents who answer the phone. These results should encourage executives to give CRM center managers the resources to ensure satisfied callers, which include employee training, coaching, and change management.

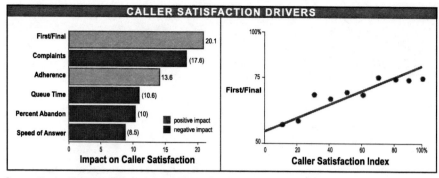

Source: Purdue University Research (published in *Call Center Magazine* July 2001)

Figures 3.5a and b. The most important customer satisfaction driver or key performance indicators are related to agents completing a customer request in one call.

Where to Spend Money

There is always the question about spending: Do we spend money on technology (hard solutions), or on people (soft solutions)? Many times leaders feel their most critical issues in business are service, quality, profitability, cost control, productivity, and overall performance. Poor performance shows up as low quality, declining profits, productivity drop-offs, sales downturns, and unacceptable customer service. And even more convincing is the fact that reduced sales and lower profits show up on the balance sheet. However, these issues represent only the symptoms of the underlying root causes. Leaders tend not to dig deeper. Part of the reason for overlooking what might really be causing the issues is the fact that leaders place more importance on "hard causes" because they seem to be based on fact. Hard causes can be debated, proven, and strategized. Yet addressing hard causes, just because they seem to be more tangible and measurable, is like being the proverbial drunk who looks futilely for his keys half a block from where he lost them, reasoning that "there isn't a street light down there." Focusing on the hard solutions because the means to address them seems clearer doesn't make the real problems go away. Ignoring the soft causes (i.e., people issues) only temporarily cures the symptoms.

In our study on agent wages we found that CRM centers that spend a greater percentage of their annual budget on better computer hardware, software, telephone equipment, and/or outsourcing tended to pay their agents less. The bracketed numbers (figure 3.5a) indicate that the higher the technology budget, the lower the hourly wage. So a well-equipped agent desktop does allow you to hire less skilled agents, who work for less money.

While it seems like finding ways to pay people less is a great strategy (because salary is a huge percentage of a company's budget), the data on hourly wage versus agent performance (average handle time) does not support that. In fact, what we found was that hourly wage has the greatest impact on average handle time. One can conclude that better paid agents, who are assumedly higher skilled, can deliver more efficient phone calls with lower handle times. (For more information on this subject, please see a complete white paper on this topic entitled "Key Performance Indicators That Drive Caller Satisfaction" at <www.Benchmarkportal.com>.)

To enhance customer service, the human capital asset is very important, and that is why it is number one in our Magic Squares for CRM implementations.

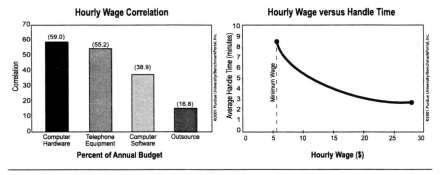

Figures 3.6a and b. (a) The more money spent on technology, the lower the agent's wages, and (b) the higher the agent's salary, the lower the average handle time.

Armed with all this data, let's now look at the subject of change management and see how it applies to technology implementations. The goal here is to understand that implementing technology means that things are going to change, and if you don't have the alignment and support of all the people in the organization, then you cannot and will not be able to satisfy your customer. Customer satisfaction is what customer obsession is all about!

Getting the People On Board with the CRM Journey

> "Change sticks when it becomes 'the way we do things
> around here.' Until new behaviors are rooted in social
> norms and shared values, they are only temporary
> and a waste of time and energy."
> —John Kotter, *Harvard Business Review*, 1995

Not doing the change part well, or at all, has significant impact
on the cost, schedule, and scope of the implementation (figure 3.7)
and, in the end, the ROI and the success of the initiative. We found
that most companies, when reviewing the budget for a technology
implementation, will spend millions of dollars on the software and
hardware, but start to cut out items like business process mapping
and reengineering. Most companies will almost always greatly reduce
or minimize the budget allocation for change management functions
like training employees or communication plans and getting "buy-in."
Technology implementations are very costly. It's wise to cut costs
where one can. Executives tend to underspend in the area of training
people to use the new, complicated technology systems. If you don't do
the change part, you risk increased scope, timelines, and budgets.

> "Today, when people say 'implement' CRM, they often
> think about technology; the reality is that you can
> only enable CRM with technology."
> —Heidi Wisbach, Manager of CRM Analytics,
> Cap Gemini Ernst and Young

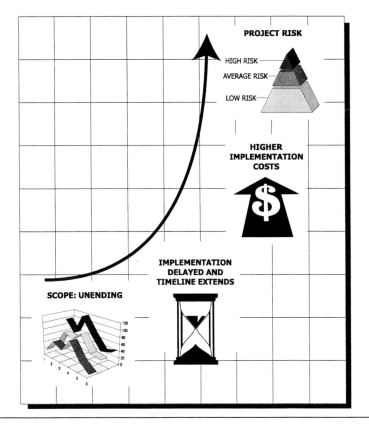

Figure 3.7. The exponential effect of not dealing with the human reaction to change is increased scope, increased costs, and missed time deadlines resulting in increased project risk and reduced ROI, as well as reduced confidence by both the employees providing the service and the customer receiving it.

In order to reduce the risks of a technology implementation, executives need to consider what to spend money on, in addition to the technology. Remember our Magic Squares in chapter 2? They include business process mapping, training, and change management (squares 1, 4, and 7.) Focusing on each of these areas will help to ensure ROI by:

- decreasing adoption resistance
  - change readiness training for human capital
  - leadership training to reduce the "Valley of Tears"
- business process mapping and reengineering
- service level agreements.

Business process design and service level agreements will be covered in the next chapter. Now let's discover the secrets to managing change.

Implementing Change Management from the Beginning

Decreasing Adoption Resistance

Employees are the ones who will be doing the planning and implementing of the new CRM system. Customers are the ones who will be using the CRM center. Thus, people (employees and customers) can affect the scope, schedule, and budget as well as the effectiveness of CRM implementations. As a result, understanding the impact of change on these two groups is important. Below is a short list of why this is so important:

1. Installing CRM means that you are going to do business differently.

2. Doing business differently means you've changed the jobs of the people who do the work, from executives to managers, to CRM center agents.

3. Changing their jobs means that employees need training to be able to do the job in the new way.

4. Once you have established a new way for the employees to provide customer service to your customers, you must communicate that to the customers who use the new system.

5. By monitoring customers reactions, incorporating their feedback, and making more changes to the technology, process, or people part of the business, you may finally gain the ROI from your CRM initiative.

Human Reaction to Change

> "It's not so much that we are afraid of change or so in love with the old ways, but it's that place in between we fear... It's like being in between trapezes. It is Linus, when his blanket is in the dryer, there's nothing to hold onto."

Change can be seen as either *crisis or opportunity*. It just depends on how it is viewed. When change is viewed as an opportunity, the exhilaration of change can be a real booster for the project. But if change is seen as a crisis, then it can be an energy sink that will sabotage and hinder the success of any CRM implementation. Whether someone sees change as a crisis or an opportunity has a lot to do with whether they are a proactive or reactive person. Forty percent of the workforce has a behavior work style that is reactive and slow to accept change. When people view change as a crisis, most things don't change. Change can be scary because it is the "unknown."

> "We've spent the majority of our energy in the 80s and 90s working on the hardware of American business because that hardware needed to be fixed. But the hardware has limits. The Japanese, on the other hand, have the culture, which ties productivity to the human spirit, which has practically no limits. That's where we have to turn to in the new millennium—to the people and the culture that drives them. We must touch every single person in the organization every business day."
> —Jack Welch, former Chairman and CEO, General Electric

To illustrate the effective use of change management, we'll look at how employees on a CRM implementation team reacted to the changes in providing service. Whether it is the CRM center agent or the head of purchasing, when technology is implemented, everyone's job changes. Change concerns everyone in the company. Figure 3.8 shows that changing how service is going to be delivered can impact their basic job functions. Figure 3.9 shows typical reactions of these employees to the changes being suggested. Many times when leaders have not led change projects, they may be surprised by the negative reactions that come from the primal part of the brain that reacts to change. This human dynamic and reaction to change, left unaddressed, is what causes implementation to go awry, increasing the project's risks.

Changing Technology and Processes Impacts The Way People Do Their Jobs

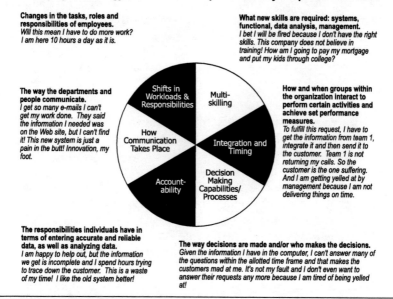

Changes in the tasks, roles and responsibilities of employees.
Will this mean I have to do more work? I am here 10 hours a day as it is.

What new skills are required: systems, functional, data analysis, management.
I bet I will be fired because I don't have the right skills. This company does not believe in training! How am I going to pay my mortgage and put my kids through college?

The way the departments and people communicate.
I get so many e-mails I can't get my work done. They said the information I needed was on the Web site, but I can't find it! This new system is just a pain in the butt! Innovation, my foot.

How and when groups within the organization interact to perform certain activities and achieve set performance measures.
To fulfill this request, I have to get the information from team 1, integrate it and then send it to the customer. Team 1 is not returning my calls. So the customer is the one suffering. And I am getting yelled at by management because I am not delivering things on time.

The responsibilities individuals have in terms of entering accurate and reliable data, as well as analyzing data.
I am happy to help out, but the information we get is incomplete and I spend hours trying to trace down the customer. This is a waste of my time! I like the old system better!

The way decisions are made and/or who makes the decisions.
Given the information I have in the computer, I can't answer many of the questions within the allotted time frame and that makes the customers mad at me. It's not my fault and I don't even want to answer their requests any more because I am tired of being yelled at!

Figure 3.8. The impact of CRM change on job functions and how people see how the change is going to affect them on a personal level

*Changing Processes and Technology Has Predictable Reactions
from the Gatekeepers: the People*

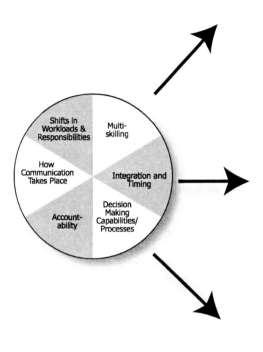

Typical Reactions

- I'm being asked to change, but what's in it for me?!
- I'm still not clear on what I'm supposed to be doing!
- I don't understand how I'm supposed to do . . .
- Why do I have to give this information to other departments? I have too much to do!
- I'm paid for production, but I have to keep stopping and entering #@!#?! data!
- What's the big deal about entering this data? We don't even use that here.
- I can't read all of this screen and I really need two screens up at once. They must have skimped on getting us the stuff we really need. What a waste of time and energy. And they wonder why morale is so low???
- This new technology was just another way to get rid of people. Another stupid decision by management and they wonder why we don't want to do this???

Figure 3.9. Typical reactions from employees who are being asked to change the way they're doing their job

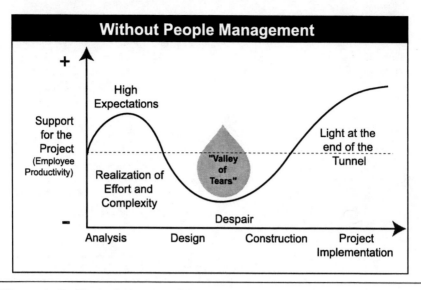

Figure 3.10. Typical emotional life cycle of a project and the level of support the CRM team gives during the various stages of implementation: analysis, design and construction. In the construction phase, teams go through what we call the "Valley of Tears."

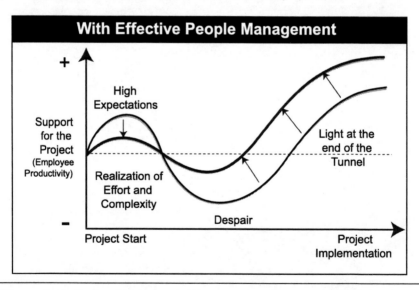

Figure 3.11. Reduction in project time and degree of the "Valley of Tears" experience with effective change management of the human potential on the teams via the CRM SSP and the corresponding information on how individuals and teams respond to change

Just as the software/hardware implementation of a CRM project has a life cycle, so does the human aspect of a project. Figure 3.10 shows a typical life cycle and the level of support the CRM team gives during the implementation. In the beginning, when the project is first announced and team members are chosen, the level of excitement and expectations is very high. As they move forward to the next stage, the amount of work the project is going to take on everyone's part starts to become clearer. Many times employees are asked not only to do the tasks required for this new project, but also to maintain the responsibilities of their current job. That in itself can send most into the despair mode, as they realize that the commitment to make the new project work and still do their other job is not only unrealistic, but personally inconvenient. They probably won't see their families for the next several months.

Near the end of a project, the light at the end of the tunnel starts to show through, and the level of support for the project increases. However, because the change was not dealt with, the net effect is that we expend more time, money, and effort. When a CRM project is led by a correctly managed change management program, it optimizes the efforts (figure 3.11), and elevates the support as seen in the life-cycle curve moving up and to the left.

Leadership Training to Reduce the Valley of the Tears

The human reaction to change was actually measured and managed at a technology implementation at Braun's CRM Center (figure 3.12) (Anton, 1998). Included are details on how the team leader and employees dealt with the various stages in the life cycle of the project and thereby increase the effectiveness and efficiency of the implementation. And most importantly, at the end of the project, people supported the CRM system. Sometimes after poorly managed implementations, teams are left with such a bad taste in their mouths that the idea of having to use the system sends them into a spin. ROI? Think again.

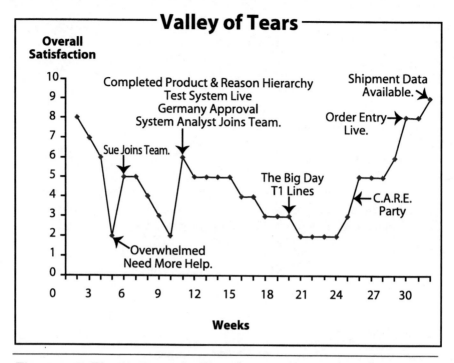

Figure 3.12. The "Valley of Tears" team experience measured during Braun's CRM implementation matches very closely with the curve that shows the theoretical response from a team over time. (Anton, 1998)

A leader's ability to lead change is dependent on mutual respect as well as human nature's reaction to change. In figure 3.13, we show the various stages of team formation and what humans experience when they have a loss. The various stages of team development are:

- ???Forming???
- !!!Storming!!!
- ...Norming...
- $$$Performing$$$
- +++Transforming +++

As a team forms and grows, team theory predicts that there will be various stages of productivity and emotions because teams are made up of people who have predictable reactions to change. Understanding these development stages can keep a team from overreacting to normal group problems and setting unrealistic group expectations that can only lead to frustration. Team theory also states that it takes a team effort to reach the performing stage of team development and to stay there. The dip in the level of

54

commitment is coined the "Valley of Tears," which describes the decline of support for the project.

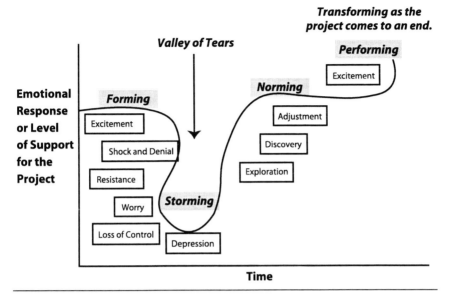

Figure 3.13. Stages of team development and stages of human loss through time

In comparing figures 3.12 and 3.13 on the "Valley of Tears," we can see that there is similarity to these graphs, which shows that theory does match reality.

In our research and reengineering experiences, we found that the "Valley" occurs regardless of the technology application or process improvement being implemented. The "Valley" happens just as commonly in implementing changes in telecommunications equipment, computer hardware, or computer software or changing the workflow or processes by which work gets done. The reason for this is because changes to technology or processes change how people do what they do at work. And remember that forty percent of the working population is adverse to change and that change in and of itself is disorienting.

In their book, *First Break All the Rules*, the Gallup Organization details the important behavioral talents that are the key to organizational success. The data is based on in-depth interviews of over 80,000 managers in over 400 companies. Their findings show those managers who focused on turning each employee's behavioral talents into superior performance had the greatest gains in productivity, job satisfaction, and retention.

Figure 3.14a shows that agents who undergo extensive (initial) training perform better on several important performance metrics. Figure 3.14b shows that agents who undergo computer based training are rewarded with better performance in several categories, namely, more calls per shift, less total training time, improved caller satisfaction, and less annual turnover rate.

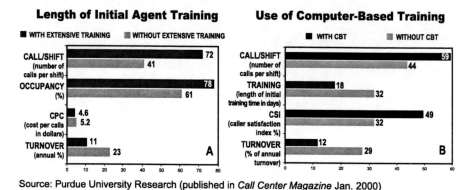

Source: Purdue University Research (published in *Call Center Magazine* Jan. 2000)

Figures 3.14a and b. (a) agents who perform better undergo extensive training, and (b) agents who have CBT perform better

In this chapter we've covered part of the necessity of squares 1, 4 and 7 in our magic squares—people and change. In the next chapter on business process design, we'll discover how including the CRM in the design phase helps to reduce the resistance of the employees in the plan, build, and maintain stages, but also the profound affect business process design has on customers and the degree to which your products and services are accessible.

Customer Obsession Graffiti #5

"Our agents tell us they feel empowered and they are handling more calls that require their skills with relevant business data in their screen pop. We are more than satisfied with the increased effectiveness of our advisers already."

—David Craggs, Head of Contact Centers, Barclays Bank

Customer Obsession Graffiti #6

We thought that the greatest merit of CTI would be on the inbound side, but outbound calls offer many opportunities for direct contact with customers."

—Mitsuharu Fukami, General Manager, Customer Service J-Phone West (Chugoku Branch)

Customer Obsession Graffiti #7

British Telephone (BT), one of the world's leading fixed/mobile communications providers, has a huge focus on customer service, publishing regular reviews of its performance, covering all aspects of its services including residential, business, services, and pay phones.

BT's call center network handles more than 80 million calls a year. "In order to handle a growing call volume here at BT, we not only needed to expand our call center operations, we also needed to make more efficient use of the call center agent resources that we already had," said Ken Brown, BT CTI Project Manager.

"By having the relevant customer information presented immediately at the start of each call, we were able to maximize the value of every call. Computer telephony helped us achieve this."

BT recognized that it needed to enable its call center agents to deal with each call more efficiently and to equip them to offer a more customer-focused service to callers. It was decided that this would, in part, be attained through benefits of a computer telephony solution, with an integrated screen pop feature.

Customers spend less time on the phone making their inquiries, but also receive a more focused service. The call center agents know who the callers are, and help them more rapidly, and should the customer need to be passed over to another agent or call center manager, there is no need to repeat the nature of their inquiry or any personal details.

—Ken Brown, BT CTI Project Manager

Understanding the Reasons for Business Process Design

In the last chapter we looked at the importance of people to the success of implementing and using CRM technology. In particular we looked at how business is accomplished by the people and the affect that adding technology can have on how employees do their job. We also saw that despite the fact that adding new technology is a wonderful step in the evolution of a business, employees can experience fear about the changes that will occur.

With the insights on people from chapter 3, in this chapter we want to focus on making a map of how business operates today. We then want to make a map of the most efficient and effective means to do business once the technology is implemented. By taking the time to design the "as is" and "could be" states of the business before ordering any hardware or software, you will be able to ensure the gains in efficiency and effectiveness by implementing the technology. Very crucial to whether you gain an ROI is whether employees are included in the business process mapping (BPM) phase. If they are included in BPM, their fears and resistance can be lessened. The reason their fears are reduced is that they have input to the changes that are going to be taking place. Having input to the changes in how they will be doing their jobs, helps them to see the advantages of the new technology, thus reducing their "pushback."

If employees have a voice in choosing the technology, they are more likely to have a vested interest in the implementation phase and will be excited about using it once it is installed. They will also be more involved and willing to go the distance during the implementation, training, and utilization phases. In cases where companies have stayed within the scope of the project, timeline and budget, they have experienced an ROI for the new CRM technology. These companies have completed the BPM step long before ever entertaining choices in software or hardware.

And as we mentioned in chapter 2, for many technology buyers the step of BPM is very different from the way most companies have bought technology in the past. While we realize this to be the case, we cannot emphasize more the need for BPM. What we find time and time again is that the technology works, but what complicates the timeline or scope is the integration of the new technology, either with existing systems or with "point solutions" from various vendors. If one does not have a map detailing where the team is starting from and where they want to end, the results of missed business goals will continue to happen. Because of the complexities of CRM, the need for integration to legacy technology, and the desire for a positive cost/benefit, BMP is a crucial step in the overall planning phase.

When business process mapping is completed, you will have a map of every customer interaction and the steps required by various employees in serving that customer. With that information, then— and only then—will you know what kind of service you want to provide. It is not enough to say, I want to increase self-service, or I want to increase e-commerce. One must decide what self-service means to you and your customers. There are literally hundreds of ways to provide self-service. You must decide—from a business point of view—what kinds of self-service would serve your customer most effectively and efficiently. With that knowledge you can then map out the steps and be able to compare options, and make informed choices of software and hardware to accomplish your business goals.

Let's take another look at our Magic Squares from chapter 2, (figure 2.3). You will see that the first, fourth, and seventh boxes are about business process mapping and business process reengineering. Yet the response of most people to the suggestion that they should map out all the processes that correspond to serving customers is met with great resistance. In fact, we hear: *"Strategy? We don't need no stinkin strategy! We need technology!"*

The typical organization seldom addresses the overall, common-sense, relationship-management strategy. More often, various strategies are developed for different scenarios by each department. The information systems (IS) department develops the Web strategy. Customer service develops the call center strategy. Nobody addresses e-mail, and what about good old-fashioned mail? Has anyone checked the mailbox lately? Meanwhile, marketing is coming up with an entirely new approach to reaching customers, but have they thought about how the customer will reach them?

The CRM strategy is important to you, as the leader. Spend time so that you know what the CRM implementation will provide with respect to customer service. Then you and your CRM implementation team need to map out what that vision means in everyday terms. If you understand what services you want to provide, it becomes clearer when you compare your "as is" and "could be" states, and where the gaps are in the following:

- Who provides the services (people)
- How the services are provided (process)
- The infrastructure by which services are delivered (technology).

When expectations are not clear, the reality of the CRM implementation is bound to be disappointing. Without assessing various technology solutions to determine if they will do what you envisioned them doing, you will not only be missing the big picture, but you'll also lack a clear understanding of all the little details that go into making the big picture happen.

In order for a CRM implementation to deliver what you dream about, it takes the ability to translate the big picture service model into the tiny details. Those tiny details determine the kind of technology you need to provide the service you want your customers to have.

Discovering the Changes That Need to be Made in How Things Are Done

Mapping out your processes (i.e., how the work gets done) is the best way to translate the big picture into the tiny details of the service process. Once you have mapped them out, then you can begin to describe the functionality that you want the software and hardware to have. This process is known as business process mapping (BPM). You may even find that you'll want to eliminate some of the steps in the process or that there are overlaps in various departments, thus leading you to do some business process reengineering (BPR). With a new look at the processes you'll use to provide service, you can then pick the technology that will really deliver this new kind of service. Most people start with telling vendors they want technology without understanding that they themselves need to understand in detail what they want that technology to do. You will want to focus on:

- handling only the high value contacts
- cost-containment through efficiencies

61

- implementing self-service options everywhere
- energizing the company's Web site to encourage more self-service
- agent-assisted service.

Accessibility versus Business Process Mapping

Let's consider the question of accessibility. You have a product that you want to sell. You want your customers to buy it from you versus your competition. The million-dollar question on accessibility is, how easy is it to do business with you—in your stores, on the Web, with an agent, via a handheld PDA, or by cell phone? Have you tried to reach your own company and buy something from them, or get a difficult question resolved via each of those touchpoints in one try? BPM is your key to enhanced accessibility. Let's see why.

The general response we get from executives is: "Of course, it is easy to do business with us. We have multiple communication channels by which our customers can reach us! Web, e-mail, fax, live agents! We have it all! Multi-channels, self-service—everything!" While that may be true, we are not asking you *what* the communication channels are, we are instead asking, *how easy is each of the channels to use?*

One of the main reasons we see a low score in accessibility is that the CEO or senior management has never used each and every touchpoint *themselves* to see if it is easy or not. Don't delegate this exercise to customer service. Do it yourself and ask each CRM implementation team member to try accessing the company through each channel and then report back what happened. When the team does this exercise and they find out what a consumer experiences, they generally turn to us and ask, now what? We respond with, business rules. You must understand your business rules. Those are the rules that govern what a customer experiences. The way the rules are discovered is by mapping out the consumer experience with each communication channel: Web, e-mail, agents, experts, PDAs, etc. Remember the goal is a customer experience that makes your customers so impressed with you that they never, ever leave you!

To really drive home this point and help you to find the motivation in your organization to do the painstaking details of BPM, let's look at a real life example. An ordinary man, Mr. Jones, calls on the morning of his wife's birthday, having forgotten to send flowers the last two years, he is again on the verge of "being in the dog house." Not to mention that he generally forgets most "Hallmark Holidays" when his wife is concerned. She happens to be born on Valentine's Day—a day when call volume is enormous. He calls 1-800 SAVE YOUR MARRIAGE. The experience of that caller, in that moment of panic, is what you want to aim for. *Can you save the day? Can your company help him before he gets relegated to the doghouse?*

Here's what the typical Mr. Jones of the world would like to experience:

"Hello, Mr. Jones. We are so happy to hear from you today. Would you like to send flowers to your wife? We see it is her birthday! How about those beautiful red and purple azaleas she ordered for herself the last three times she called. And I see you have booked a weekend away for the both of you. We can reserve dinner at the hotel for you. We can schedule a scuba diving trip and rent the equipment as well. We see she has been surfing our scuba shop Web site and we can tell you exactly what she has been looking at versus what she has already purchased. We also have a special on fishing poles, if you would like to get a deep-sea fishing pole for yourself. And one more thing, Mr. Jones, we have a special on diamond necklaces. This is your 20th anniversary and this necklace is very popular gift. It was given a rating of 95% in our customer service polls from women who received this gift on their "diamond" anniversary. If you log on to our site, we can browse through some other items you might want to consider together. Now, let's get started Mr. Jones! What is your first item?"

In one call, the birthday weekend and trip are handled. Mr. Jones can go back to what he does at work, which is manage a demanding group of corporate accounts. The best news? Mr. Jones won't be sleeping in the doghouse tonight. Customer for life? You bet!

Instead of the experience Mr. Jones had with 1-800 SAVE YOUR MARRIAGE, table 4.1 shows what the consumer often experiences when a company has not checked how accessible their products and services are via technology.

Table 4.1. Typical Consumer Experience

Consumer Action	Consumer Experience	Possible Cause(s) of Problem
Dials the number.	Call gets dropped.	CTI or IVR failed to connect to mainframe database
Dials again.	Gets a busy signal.	Blocked trunk lines
Dials again.	Gets an IVR with 10 choices. Can't remember all the choices so he asks the IVR to repeat the choices again.	• Poorly designed IVR menu • Misdirected call flow
Selects one of the menu choices.	It is not the right thing, so he asks the IVR to repeat the choices again.	Poorly designed IVR menu
Selects another menu choice and then zeros out to an agent.	Gets transferred to an agent and has to wait; told the wait time is 10 minutes. Decides to try the Web site.	• Poor agent queuing • Lack of workforce management • Programming errors in IVR call flow • Lack of planning for holiday call load
Logs onto the Web site.	Takes a long time for the site to load. He goes to get a coffee and someone tells him of another site that is great. He makes mental note of to shop elsewhere.	Poorly designed Web site
Web site loads, but he isn't sure where the stuff for women is.	He searches 5 different areas, but can't find where the flowers are.	Poorly organized Web layout
He finds the section to order the flowers, but now what else should he get? Travel? Other presents?	He searches further, but he has opened so many pages, finally finding the gifts and travel. He is not sure how to make dinner reservations, so he skips that and goes onto other gifts. Then he wishes he could remember where the jewelry was he saw early. He looks at his watch. He clicks on the button for an agent. The wait time is 10 minutes. He has 20 minutes before his next meeting.	• Poorly organized Web layout • Poor access to agent assisted self-service
He calls another company who truly has integrated all their customer service and places the order.	**He gets everything done in one call and one visit to the Web site.**	**No problems in customer service or accessibility via technology-IVR, Web, etc.**

64

The point of the birthday example is to drive home the importance of the *experience the customer* has with your company. That experience is dependent on the business rules with which your company provides services to your customer. If you have not thought about those rules or mapped them out to see the holes in them, your customer experience could be very similar to the one in table 4.1. Another example is self-service which, if done well, can provide for a less expensive customer interaction than a call to an agent. However, if the self-service is not done well, the customer either goes to a competitor or ends up calling the agent for help. Making self-service *truly service* requires that one really sit in the seat of the user and experience how it feels to use the technology. If it does not feel good, the customer will leave. End of story.

The following are self-service questions to ask yourself and the CRM team that will define the BPM, and guide the technology choice:

- Is it easy?

- Is it clear?

- Is it intuitive?

- Does it take a long time?

- Are there many steps?

- Does it feel satisfying enough that you would want to use it again and again and again?

When it does not feel good, the tendency for customers is to hang up or log off and contact a competitor, never to return again. To avoid that happening to your customers, we cannot emphasize enough the need for businesses to map out every touchpoint and combination of touchpoints a customer can experience and then build business rules around them. From the map you can then determine what technology can deliver the experience you want the customer to have. Keep in mind, the more sophisticated the experience, the more it will cost and the longer it can take to implement and integrate. However, many times that upfront investment will serve you and those customers for years to come.

Functionality Point Analysis

Functionality point analysis is a term used by software engineers to determine the functions one wants to have versus what would be required of the technology to provide that experience. The technology required to provide excellent customer service falls into various categories:

- Operational CRM
- Analytical CRM
- Collaborative CRM
- E-Commerce CRM
- Supply Chain CRM.

We will cover technology in detail in chapter 5, but for now let's continue to focus on mapping out your business processes, risk management, and functional point analysis.

If you analyze the business requirements to provide each step to serve the customer, then you will know what you want the software and hardware to do. This is known as "functionality point analysis" which means that for every point of functionality, there is something the software or hardware must do to make that happen. And there is a cost structure associated with each piece of technology providing service, as shown in figure 4.1 (Anton, 2001).

Cost Structure of Customer Service

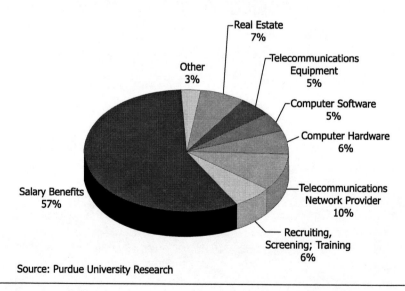

Source: Purdue University Research

Figure 4.1. Cost structure versus technology choices

What you should also know is that there is a cost associated with each point of functionality. Every time you say, "Gosh, it would be great if the customer could…," know that—unless this is a standard part of the software/hardware solution—you are adding more work and cost (figure 4.2).

Make sure that you have your technologist talk to the technology integrator to avoid the issue of overselling functionality in the sales process by the vendor. It is very difficult to compare one vendor to another because each vendor has a different set of functions as part of the standard package and others that are extra. Vendors have not done this to be purposefully confusing, but rather, each vendor's technical staff has developed their technology on a different set of assumptions. The result is that certain items are standard practice for them and others require additional work.

Each vendor includes different levels of functionality in their standard product package versus upgrades. Differences in functionality can be a big reason why it is so difficult to make an "apples to apples" comparison between software or hardware vendors. What you must understand, with the help of your CIO and IS department, is if what you are asking for is standard or if it will cost extra. Figure 4.2 shows that 80% of today's volume of customer service inquiries is in the lower left hand part of the graph. Use this as a reminder to ask your team if you really need this or if you can accomplish what your true business goals are without it. You may find that each piece of hardware and software is necessary to carry out your customer service strategy. In other cases you might find that it is an item that is "nice to have, but not necessary" or it might be something you would want to add in the future. If it is something that you plan on adding, then it is important to make sure it will integrate with everything else in your plan.

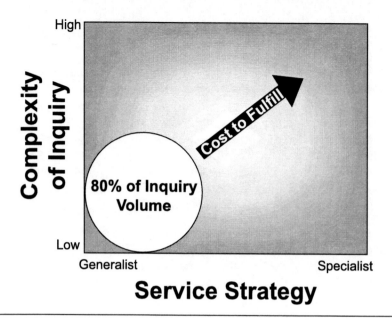

Figure 4.2. Complexity of inquiry and service strategy

If each functionality point is discussed and weighed up-front, then the risk in performance versus cost, timeline, and scope can easily be determined. Many times you will want to spend the extra money to have the functionality, but you will be doing this with your eyes wide open. Figure 4.3 shows the issue of increased functionality (information and control systems) and cost per seat. If you learn to evaluate the choices of technology versus functionality and cost, there will be no surprises, slipped scope, or timelines.

Figure 4.4 shows the competing demands of:

* customer expectations
* minimum, desired and ideal service quality standards
* competitors quality/performance, and
* price.

The *"keeping up with the Jones"* mentality of many companies is fed by what we call the customer expectation inflation cycle. The exponential rise in customer expectations is being driven by the competing demands of competitor quality, price and performance, on one hand, and your own customer service quality standards on the other. Sometimes the upward spiral is being driven artificially, hence the *keep up with the Jones,* decision-making results.

The way to avoid getting swept away by the whirlwind of hype, is to understand who your customers are, the services you want to provide, and how you want to provide them. You will then be able to determine "how good is good enough," and not overspend on technologies with diminishing returns. Only buy what accomplishes your business objectives. Make that technology work for you and then, revaluate your strategy and business process to determine if you want to add more. But only add more if it makes good business sense. Otherwise you will join the 55% of CRM buyers who spent too much and did not reach their business objectives.

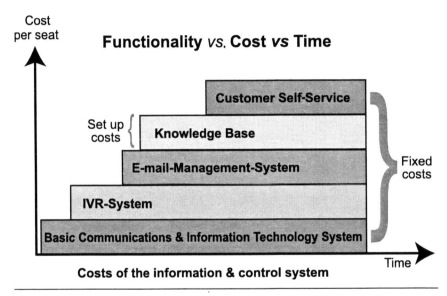

Figure 4.3. This graph shows the comparison of the increased functionality (information and control systems) and cost / seat.

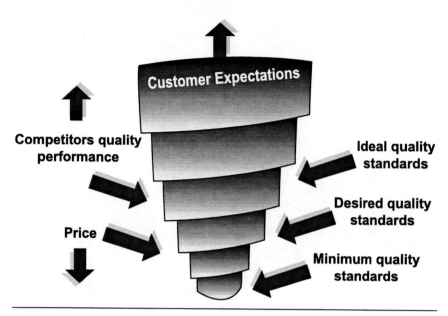

Figure 4.4. Balancing between customer expectations and true business needs of today

You and your team now have a method for creating proactive choices for your business. You now understand why it is important to determine who your customers are and what their expectations are as the criteria for determining how much functionality you actually need.

Figure 4.5 compares the financial impact of various technology channel alternatives. Telephoning agents are the most expensive channel, whereas Web-self-service is the least. If your customers don't have push-button phones (in some parts of the world this is the case), then an IVR may not make sense. Make sure that you do not make decisions based on what other companies have. Make decisions on what will serve your most profitable customers the best that you can. In chapter 7 we will explore customer segmentation and how to target your most profitable customers in more detail.

Comparing the Financial Impact of Alternatives

CRM Channel	Average Cost per Transaction
Telephone	$12.56
E-mail	$8.79
Web Chat	$4.62
Web self-service	$0.76

Figure 4.5. The financial impact of various technology channel alternatives from research done at BenchmarkPortal

Defining your Vision for the "Could Be" CRM Center

To define the vision for the future, it is important to outline the current processes that the technology supports and to map the changes to the process that new technology would create. The following are examples of a variety of ways to map out the various processes in a business that provides service. Figure 4.6 is a very simplified version of a business process map showing the "as is" and the "could be" states of an employee needing to change data such as an address or marital status. With the old system, there are many steps, and with the new self-service technology, those steps can be reduced.

71

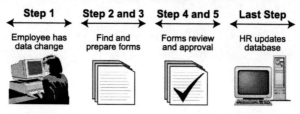

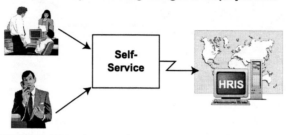

Figure 4.6. The "as is" and "could be" states of service in an HR department

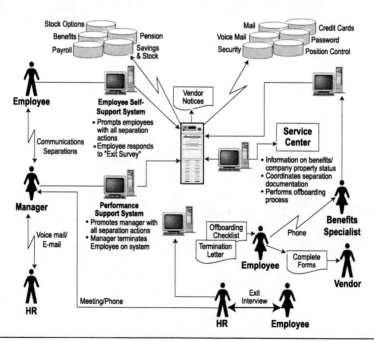

Figure 4.7. Business process map of the steps in a company when an employee quits his/her job

Figure 4.7 is a business process map of the steps in a company when an employee quits his/her job. In this process map, there are three main human touchpoints: the employee or colleague, the manager, and HR. There are numerous processes and technologies that support the process of an employee quitting.

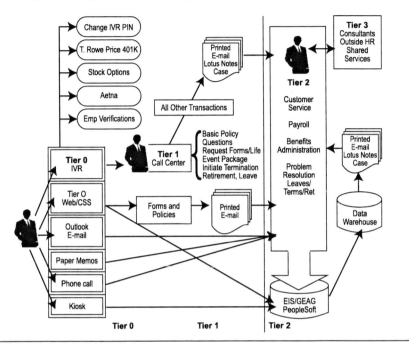

Figure 4.8. Business process map of the different tiers in delivering service to customers

Figure 4.8 is a business process map of the different tiers in delivering service to customers. Tier 0 is self-service. Tier 1 is the call center. Tier 2 refers to when questions are escalated to a specialist in the call center, and tier 3 is when an HR consultant becomes involved. This company wanted to reduce the number of interactions in tiers 1 to 3 and increase the volume of providing service via tier 0 or self-service technology. It was not until this company mapped out their service delivery model that they were able to see what they wanted to change and why it would reduce costs. Now that we have looked at the various aspects of BPM, let's look at measuring and managing the success we created.

Service Level Agreements

So you want to set up the best CRM program in your industry and you just:

- reduced the adoption resistance
- mapped out all your processes
- removed extra steps by BPR
- bought technology that enables your people and processes.

After all the benchmarking, planning, and changing, what happens, if along the way, a department manager or a call center agent doesn't do what they said they would? You can have all the pieces of CRM in place, but without a solid agreement on who is going to manage what, by when, with specific measurements, the chances of having and maintaining a successful CRM implementation decreases dramatically with each passing day. Producing *exceptional* quality customer service remains an unattainable goal, not a reality to your staff. The time spent on BPM ends up being a waste of energy if there is not an agreement to manage the process and change. Your competitive edge becomes status quo. Your company becomes one of the pack. Your level of service looks no different than your competitors. And, as a result, the return on your investment for technology is far less than you expected.

Historically clients tend to roll their eyes at the mention of service level agreements (SLAs) in facilitating CRM. When we asked why service level agreements got a negative response, we were told that many times these documents were never referenced again after first being written. Staff who did the actual fulfillment of SLAs are typically not included in the level setting nor reminded of the metrics or changes made to service levels.

Another client said that, unless the whole company is involved and committed to using the service agreements, all it takes is one weak link in the chain to bring down a service level percentage. There is nothing to be gained from advertising your inability to meet service levels. And then finger pointing begins. There is no accountability. It turns into a "they promised and did not deliver" mudslinging match. Traditionally the answer has been to write the service-level metrics into performance appraisals, to be used as criteria for raises and bonuses. This is a management option that too often is not utilized, because the nature of some fast-moving customer service centers may be based on hitting daily targets as opposed to quarterly goals.

74

Keeping written performance appraisals up-to-date in these environments is not practical.

Another important issue with service levels that came up in talking to clients was accountability. What we found in service level agreements that did work was that they were in organizations that had people dedicated full time to making sure the service levels were managed. When companies did not have at least two people—a director level and support staff—dedicated to this process, the responsibility of engaging in service-level discussions at the staff level often fell through the cracks. This was because, on top of someone's regular job, they were assigned extra duty to capture data and manage the reporting needed to maintain service level agreements. What some management did not understand was that it was a full-time job to have someone manage the quality process of service levels.

In this chapter we have covered the reasons why you will want to map out your business processes and reexamine your choices for technology selection. In the next chapter we will take an in-depth look at the process of technology selection. You will be provided tools that will enable you to make better decisions and gain higher return on investments.

Customer Obsession Graffiti #8

"If you're building a house to last, you need a foundation first—that's what CTI is. Once you've got that, you can add anything—e-commerce, workforce management, multimedia and CRM."

—*CTI Application Team Manager, Verizon*

Customer Obsession Graffiti #9

Customer service in the past has been the realm of the telephone, where typical centers handle nothing but phone calls. As these new channels of communication come into play, companies are facing increased demands on their customer service organizations.

Sento's Technical Services group provides outsourced product support for software developers and hardware manufacturers.

"You start attracting a more computer-literate user who wants to use e-mail, the phone, Web call back, text chat and tools like that. So companies that are purely telephone-centric are going to have a problem," says Sento marketing manager Robert Sorenson.

"There is no doubt that we have to respond to the growth in the Internet," adds Keith Barr, Chief Information Officer. "That means direct Web interactions as well as e-mail or text type chat communications. Our objective was to differentiate ourselves by providing better service through technology."

Sento changed switch platforms and introduced a new interaction management architecture into their new customer contact center. Sento refers to their agents as technicians because of their expertise in high-tech support.

Sento's response times now averages less than five minutes. Their Web site touts: "No other support center in the world can match our speed and efficiency."

—*Robert Sorenson, Sento Marketing Manager*

Introduction to Technology Strategy

In chapter 2 we discussed how a CRM technology implementation does not always achieve its business objective and that this was especially true when the strategy was flawed from the beginning. We asked executives in various industries whether they felt that the CRM center was a way to manage customer value. Figure 5.1 shows the various industries versus the relative opportunity to manage customer value via the CRM center. In all cases, regardless of industry, the conclusion was yes, CRM implementation is related to managing and improving customer value.

We also interviewed executives to determine what they considered to be the most important element for success in a CRM implementation initiative. In figure 5.2 we see that only 1.8% selected CRM corporate strategy as a critical success factor. This is a critical data point in that we have found that lack of a coherent strategy is the formula for disappointment in CRM implementation.

In this chapter, we provide you with criteria to create a practical technology strategy so that your CRM project will achieve the targeted ROI potential.

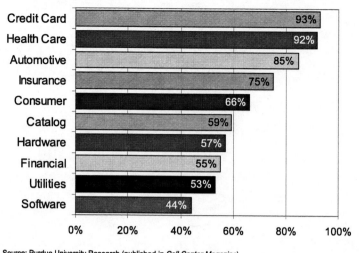

Source: Purdue University Research (published in *Call Center Magazine*)

Figure 5.1. Relative opportunities to manage customer value via the CRM center

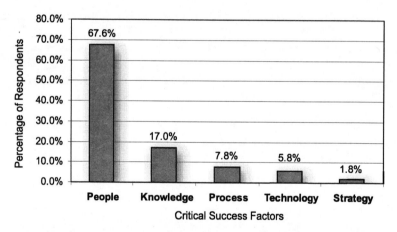

Source: Purdue University Research (published in *Call Center Magazine*)

Figure 5.2. CRM center critical success factors

Our years of research and practical experience in implementing technology have enabled us to aid CEOs, CIOs, COOs, and CFOs in avoiding CRM disasters, and in creating business strategies that are synergistically aligned to the technology strategy.

Starting With What You Have

Step one is evaluating your current CRM center to determine what, if any, changes need to be made with respect to technology strategy, business objectives, and technology purchases. We suggest again that you benchmark your CRM center to get a baseline. With that baseline, begin to evaluate your next steps. Later in this chapter we will give you technology selection matrices to help you sort out the dilemma of prioritizing technology selections.

By starting with the CRM center, each deployed channel can then benefit from the integrated knowledge management environment resulting in consistency of service across all channels and improved agent productivity. Your company can be successful at transforming the CRM center into a multi-channel CRM center, but there are many things that you need to consider in order for that to happen. We will go into more detail later in this chapter on what our research has shown as important issues to consider.

Inventory Existing Technology

Before adding new technology, you will want to inventory the technology you currently have and decide whether to start from scratch or to leverage prior investments. For your company to capitalize on the business opportunities made possible by the Internet—and migrate your CRM center to a multimedia CRM center—you must first determine the degree to which you can leverage legacy systems versus embarking on a wholesale infrastructure rebuild. When choosing to leverage existing technology, you will want to choose systems that easily integrate with and leverage your existing business systems. This process is known as reengineering. Within this context, four principal areas need to be considered:

- Identifying whether your CRM center functionality—such as ACD, IVR, and CTI—should remain premises-based, as opposed to migrating these capabilities to the network.

- Developing a mechanism for establishing consistent business rules for contact handling across multiple channels.

- Re-evaluating your deployment of related applications such as CRM in a multimedia environment.

- Ensuring that CRM center reporting and analysis capabilities keep pace as new interaction channels are introduced.

79

CRM Center Reengineering

The traditional CRM center infrastructure includes ACD, IVR, and CTI platforms as well as interfaces to back-office resources such as databases and to front-office applications such as desktop information systems. In most cases, this infrastructure was not engineered upfront as a collective entity. Rather, various systems were brought together over time as your company introduced new technologies to reduce costs, improve customer service, or both.

Some questions to ask your potential vendors are:

- Can the integration with business systems be done quickly, and is it easy to set up using a forms-based configuration?

- Can integration enable agents to view relevant information when servicing customers? For example, would integrating with a system enable agents to pull up the details of a customer order? Integrating with shipping systems would enable agents to access the shipping status for a customer.

- Can integration also be used for routing customers and responding to inquiries? For example, when a customer requests service, information received from an external integrated system can be used to determine where to route the customer. Would that enable your business to give premium customers the priority service they have earned?

The advent of the multimedia CRM center offers businesses a unique opportunity to rationalize and define the overall blueprint for customer interaction. Let's examine some of the more significant areas for consideration as your traditional CRM center migrates from standalone voice and IVR silos to multiple channels across multiple locations.

Premises Versus Network

Overall, premises-based, contact-processing platforms are today being outmaneuvered by network-based solutions and deployments. As new media types are brought into the CRM center, as voice and data silos give way to an enterprise architecture, and as agents become skilled in multiple channels, the traditional, premises-based approach to ACD and IVR becomes cost-prohibitive and presents scaling challenges. In this way, Internet-based customer contact channels are driving the adoption of network-hosted ACD and IVR capabilities to ensure scalability and to deliver multimedia,

80

enterprise-wide prompting, routing, and processing of customer contacts. Likewise, network CTI moves the traditionally premised-based qualification and routing components of CTI to the network level. Going forward, network CTI will provide qualification and routing across multiple contact channels from a network-based platform, with real-time visibility into multiple agent queues across multiple locations.

Customer Relationship Management

CRM is rapidly emerging as a key component of customer-contact strategy, especially as it pertains to customer lifecycle management. To ensure success in a multimedia, enterprise-wide CRM center environment, a solution must support real-time profiling for qualification, routing, and treatment based on up-to-date information housed in a common data repository.

Reporting and Analysis

It is critical that your CRM center engineering process include an evaluation of reporting and analysis capabilities early on in the overall technology design. Ultimately, the data provided by the reporting/analysis application will enable you to generate business metrics including acquisition cost, percent retention or loss, cross-selling, up-selling, and channel performance.

CRM Center Architecture

Once you've addressed the issues reflected in the CRM center engineering process, you'll need to assess the infrastructure implications of the decisions you've made. The customer-contact network will increasingly be IP-based for all media types including voice. This means that real-time, multimedia qualification can now take place at a single point in the network with real-time routing to your entire base of live agents and other answering resources. Service levels can be dramatically improved and costs reduced by utilizing resources across your entire enterprise.

Consistent Contact Handling

As the traditional call center migrates to the multimedia CRM center, companies should expect increased demand for select media types such as e-mail and Web collaboration, as well as a melding of delivery channels. For example, a Web chat session can move quickly into Web collaboration with the sharing of Web pages between agent and caller. Even more dramatic, Web collaboration and voice interaction can be initiated from e-mails sent to prospects and customers simply by including an appropriate link! As customers increasingly expect to interact with your company via the channel of their choosing—and in some cases via multiple channels during a single session—decisions must be made about database deployment and architecture.

Traditionally, the CRM center has maintained a customer-profile database to support real-time profiling, treatment, and routing of voice calls and IVR transactions. As new contact channels are introduced, you will need to decide whether it makes better sense to maintain niche databases by media type or a general-purpose data repository across channels. You should consider the architectural and support ramifications of maintaining separate databases for each media type versus a single, enterprise-wide, multimedia profiling system.

The steps in your CRM life cycle plan are:

1. **Establish CRM Direction**—Develop a comprehensive plan for implementing your multimedia CRM center enterprise including a roadmap for technology upgrades.

2. **Deliver Quick Wins**—Establish an interdisciplinary project team with a demonstrated track record. Be sure to include contact center agents—the folks who will ultimately implement the plan!

3. **Evolve to Integrated Model**—From your plan, evolve in a phased implementation to a fully integrated system.

4. **Measure and Tune**—Establish metrics specific to your company and a corresponding cost/benefit analysis model.

At the onset of any major project to Web-enable your CRM center, remember this: your existing technology infrastructure may have developed organically and/or you may be quite comfortable with it, but now you have the opportunity to truly engineer a new infrastructure! Do it right and your business can begin reaping the customer loyalty and profitability benefits that come with riding the Internet wave.

Understanding Urgency Versus Importance When Deciding What To Do First

Our second step is to help you prioritize the technology selections. Two technology selection matrices will be covered in this section.

82

Figure 5.3 is a matrix that shows the various options when choosing which solution to implement first. The best way to use this graphic is to understand the urgency versus the importance of the technology solution.

The things to consider in selecting solutions that address both urgency and importance regarding your CRM center are:

1. Focus on those issues that negatively impact cost containment.

2. Focus on those issues that negatively impact revenue.

3. Focus on those issues that create more telephone calls or e-mails.

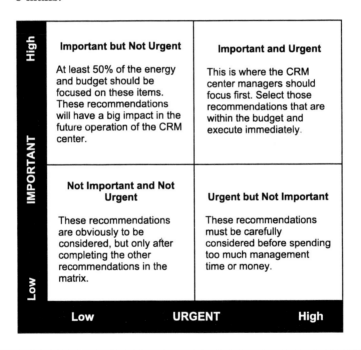

*Figure 5.3. **Urgency** versus **importance** of the solution matrix*

Understanding the Ease of Implementation Versus the Impact When Deciding the Order of CRM-enabling Technology Implementation

The next step is to understand the difference between *ease of implementation* versus the *impact* the technology will have on the business results (see figure 5.4). In selecting solutions that address both *"impact"* and *"ease of implementation"* regarding your CRM center, consider the following:

1. Focus on solutions that are relatively easy to implement, yet have a major impact on center performance.

2. Focus on solutions that are easy to integrate with existing technology.

3. Focus on solutions that have a major impact on productivity of the human element in a center, i.e., the most expensive part of your center.

4. Focus on solutions where the vendor has "validated" that the product has a measurable impact on the performance of your center.

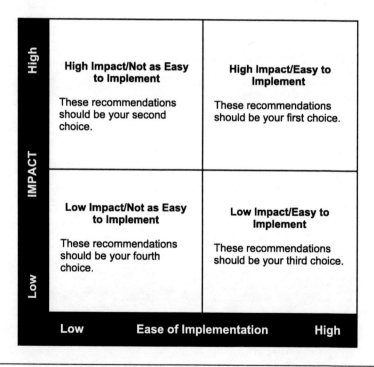

Figure 5.4. **Ease of implementation** *versus the* **impact of technology** *matrix*

A Roadmap of CRM-enabling Technology Implementation

The evolution of customer service from a phone-dominated medium to a multi-channel medium has led to many challenges that need to be addressed. Here are some of the most important points we have found:

- Evolution means change and change leads to risk if not properly managed. Companies cannot afford to make changes to the customer service environment in a manner that causes disruption to the current service environment.

- Agents need to be able to find up-to-date answers quickly for customers. During the evolution to multiple service channels, up-to-date answers can become more difficult to find if answers are updated without making the updates easy to access for all agents across all channels.

- As channels are added, agent expertise needs to be replicated so the correct answers can be delivered regardless of the channel through which the customer chooses to make contact.

- Increasing customer service expectations are a driver of the multi-channel evolution, but service budgets are limited. Increasing customer expectations must be met cost-effectively.

- Customers need to be trained to use the new service channels so that they can be effectively utilized.

- As customers become able to make contact more easily with companies, they will. Skyrocketing levels of customer inquiries must be managed in order to ensure timely responses are received.

- Providing poor service in any one channel will impact the reputation of the company as a whole. Maintaining quality of service across all channels is critical.

- For maximum success, the change from phone service to multi-channel service should be a service evolution, not revolution. So prior investments in the service environment should be leveraged.

A phased approach that minimizes the risk of evolving from a call center to a multi-channel CRM center is required to effectively and efficiently gain the competitive edge that a multi-channel customer service project can bring to the company. It is better to do one or two

85

customer touchpoints very well than to do ten poorly. The effect of ten poorly deployed channels is that no matter how your customer tries to communicate with you, they will all be perceived as failures and result in customer loss. If you do one to three very well, you will be able to retain those customers and add new ones as you add more communication channels.

A CRM-enterprise solution consists of multiple components that enable companies to deliver superior service via the phone and e-mail, and through the Web site with live online assistance and Web self-service. Knowledge must be integrated across all channels to ensure consistency of answers. Bridges and gateways or routing can be used to integrate the solution with existing systems enabling them to be leveraged for delivering superior service. You will want to consider an integrated solution that easily adapts to changing environments and provides a system where:

- Modularity enables components to be deployed as needed.
- Scalability through a Web-native architecture and support for Unix platform means that you won't outgrow the ability to handle the growing number of customers that delivering superior service brings.
- Multi-lingual support enables businesses to easily deliver service in a global environment.
- Deployment is flexible with the availability of solutions for Windows and Unix and in a hosted or licensed environment.
- Integration with existing and future systems is no problem with support for EJB, COM, JDBC, HTML, and XML.

As we have said before, the first step is to improve the communications within the existing CRM center environment. Not only does this result in a quicker return on the investment, it also makes the move to a multi-channel CRM center much smoother.

Next, Web self-service can be used to improve service while reducing service costs. Service can be improved by empowering customers to find answers 24x7 in an efficient and personalized manner. Service costs are reduced by enabling customer inquiries to be resolved without the need to call an agent for help.

Online assisted-service is used by agents to help customers migrate to the self-service environment. Just giving customers the URL to the self-service environment isn't enough to make them comfortable using it instead of calling. But if an agent shows them the environment and what they can do there, they will be much more likely to use it in the future instead of calling for help. E-mail interactions are proactively managed, ensuring that customers receive fast and accurate service via e-mail—even when inquiry volumes are skyrocketing. As each channel is added to the service mix, consistency and high quality of service is maintained across all service channels.

Minimizing the Risk of a CRM-enabling Technology Implementation

Here are important aspects to consider when using the technology selection matrix to minimize risk:

- Consistency of answers is maintained through centralized knowledge that is accessible by agents and customers across all channels of contact.

- Supervisors have the tools they need to monitor agent communications and to assist them when they need to ensure accuracy. They can analyze self-service transcript reports to identify when changes need to be made to the self-service environment or the Web site.

- Supervisors can also analyze activity reports that provide them with the information they need to analyze response timeliness and to effectively schedule agents.

- Customers can be surveyed across channels to determine the effectiveness of the service they received.

- Surveys can be automatically sent to customers via e-mail, given by agents online, or even given by the virtual assistant online.

- Making surveys easily accessible to customers not only helps to increase the customer service feedback that is received, it also indicates that the company cares about the level of service the customer receives.

Routing as an Enabler of Superior Customer Service

If the items above are important to you—and they should be—then you will also want to look at the option of routing (see figure 5.5). In today's demanding customer market, the CIO's focus will most likely be on enabling:

- customer segmentation
- self-service
- channel integration.

The Yankee Group reports that routing is the only way that the above agendas can truly be accomplished (Mello, 2002). Their research shows the market trend is:

- separation of queuing and routing frameworks from dedicated platforms with more emphasis on management of not just interactions, but also post-interaction workflow tasks, greater use of analytics to enhance profiling and real-time interaction management, and

- greater involvement of CRM front-office vendors in the interaction management process.

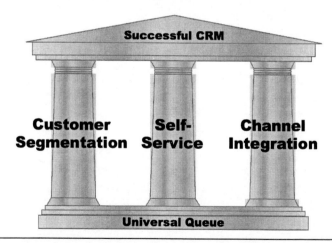

Figure 5.5. Successful CRM and a universal queue

How Routing Helps Customer Segmentation

If you are trying to do CRM with finite resources, the most important aspect of CRM is to segment your customer via their value to you. In order to accomplish the competing goals of retaining

88

customers, expanding markets, and improving efficiencies, you need to **know your customer**. You will then be able to:

- profile customers based on their contribution to profits
- interact differently with high- versus low-value customers
- turn every interaction into customer insight.

The best way to expand market, retain customers, and improve efficiencies is to segment your customer interactions (see figures 5.6 and 5.7).

Routing interactions based on customer profiles allows you to (a) select the optimal resource or channel, and (b) leverage up-sell opportunities, thereby turning every interaction into customer insight. The importance of this type of interaction cannot be stressed more. The opportunity is there because nine out of every ten interactions are not transactions but some form of communication. The challenge is knowing how to successfully transform the communication into a sale. This can be accomplished if you know your customer.

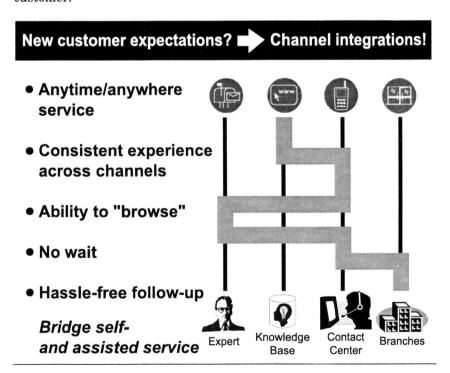

Figure 5.6. Channel integration

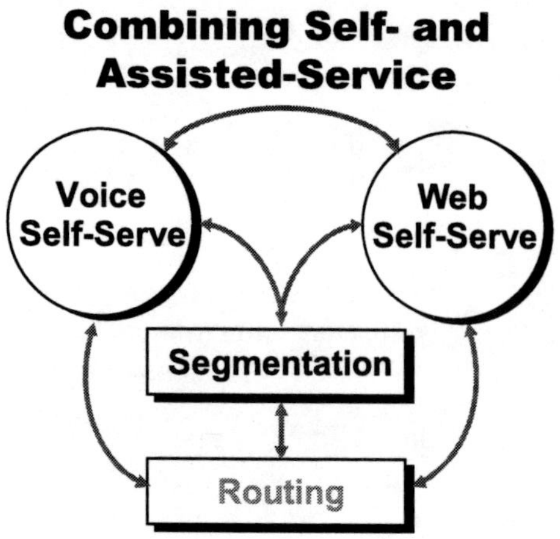

Combining Self- and Assisted-Service

Figure 5.7. The synergistic relationship of combined self- and assisted-service via routing

How Routing Helps Self-Service

Here are some examples of why you will want to consider multi-channels, especially self-service:

- 12% of business in Sears stores is a result of research at Sears Online.

- 50% of Web interactions take place over the phone.

- 67% transaction revenue increase is realized when a customer service agent gets on the phone.

- 70% of new Schwab customers join via its branch offices, but make nearly 90% of their trades over the Internet. At the same time, the company's CRM centers handle more than 10 million calls per month.

- 90% of BMW North America's customers use the Internet before making their final decision to buy a new BMW.

Routing enables self-service by allowing for agent-assisted self-service. Take, for instance, figure 5.6, where the interaction of a customer with various customer touchpoints is shown. If the customer is searching the Web and has a pivotal question that can be answered easily by an agent, then the likelihood of the customer to buy is greatly enhanced. Channel integration allows the customer to interface with you based on their needs, not yours. Our research shows that customer interaction is very situational. For instance, customers driving in their cars most likely will not be logging on to your Web site. But if they can get a question answered while sitting in traffic, when they arrive at their destination they are more motivated to log on and order without hesitation. Whether it is via e-mail, the Web, the phone, or at your store, you will want your customer to be able to access you easily.

How Routing Helps Channel Integration

Now let's explore channel integration. If you want to combine self- and assisted-service, figure 5.7 shows how routing is the key. Figure 5.8 shows how business intelligence and analysis and planning with enterprise resources can be combined with the various customer touchpoints. If you just want to transfer the call via an ACD, then a standard ACD will work fine. However, if you want to collect data, manage by business rules, use logic in the call routing, and increase quality, then one-to-one routing is required. If you are considering a routing solution, here is a list of questions to ask your vendor. We recommend choosing a routing company that is:

- enterprise-ready (scalability, availability, and references), and
- IP telephony ready.

The vendor should be capable of:

- supporting all touchpoints (voice and Internet)
- supporting legacy infrastructure (IVR and switches)
- tying multiple sites and remote workers into virtual centers
- packaging integration with front-office applications
- providing proactive contact management
- collecting data from every interaction
- seamless integration of self- and assisted-services
- enabling business routing
- resource optimization (scheduled and real-time).

The best way to channel integrate is to:

- route interaction based on customer/context
- link interaction portions across channels
- bridge self- and assisted-service
- enable proactive contact
- track from cradle to grave to anywhere beyond the contact center.

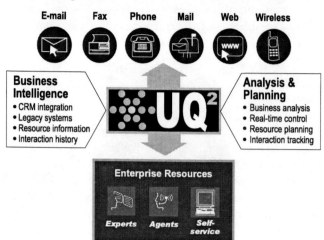

Figure 5.8. Multi-channel, value-based CRM requires a way to queue all the information from business intelligence, analysis and planning, and enterprise resources.

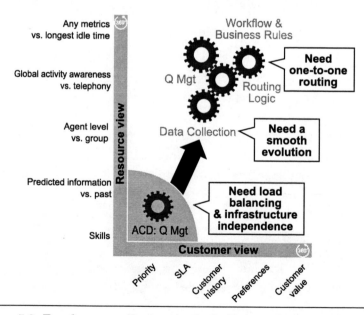

Figure 5.9. For the most effective method of accomplishing the business objectives—collecting data, managing by business rules, using logic in the call routing and increasing quality—one to one routing is required.

Open Technology Platforms

Characteristics of service that influences how positive the customer experience is should include consistency, accuracy, timeliness, and effectiveness. Enterprise CRM enables companies to excel at these characteristics across all service channels as they are added to the service mix so a superior level of customer service can be delivered—no matter how the customer chooses to make contact. In order to accomplish this, the choice of technology is critical. Figure 5.10 shows the possibility for expansion when an open platform is used.

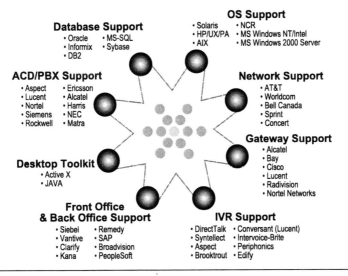

Figure 5.10. Open platforms and CRM technology strategy

Various Types of Technology and Issues to Consider

With our research at Purdue University in best practices, we are approaching a database of 8,000 CRM centers. With this datamart we are able to research the implementation rates of specific technology solutions. In table 5.1, we listed the ten generic technologies known to all CRM center managers. The table shows the percentage of participating CRM centers that have the technologies installed, that are planned, and that are still undecided. This datamart is comprised only of North American companies. In comparing that data to data from Japan (see figure 5.11), we see that there is a range of CRM technology implementation throughout the world. In some countries, CRM is standard practice while in others it is an emerging market.

Table 5.1. Technology Implementation Status

Technology Implementation
in percent

Technology	In Place	Planned	Undecided
Interactive Voice Response	56	22	22
Agent Monitoring	39	21	40
Analytic Toolset	31	12	57
Workforce Management	29	18	53
Computer Telephony Integration	23	18	35
Skill-Based Routing	18	10	72
Reader Boards	17	8	75
Customer Interaction Mgmt	7	24	69
Outsourcing Calls	6	15	79
Voice Over Internet Protocol	1	18	81

Source: Purdue University Research (published in *Call Center Magazine* Sept. 2000)

Implementation of CRM in Japan

No plans to implement
51.5%

Already implemented
9.1%

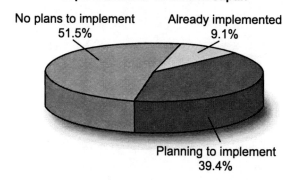

Planning to implement
39.4%

Nearly 90% of Companies in Japan
Have Yet to Implement CRM

Source: IDC Japan, 2001 © 2002 Genesys Telecommunications Laboratories, Inc.

Figure 5.11. Percentage of companies in Japan that have implemented CRM

Computer Telephony Integration

From the Purdue research (figure 5.12), we inquired about CRM center managers' experience with computer telephony integration software (CTI). Our research shows that only 11% felt that the CTI worked better than expected. Nearly 18% would like to have CTI, but do not have the budget allocated for it. When we see this kind of result, it is generally because the CEO or CFO does not understand the connection between CTI and channel integration, customer segmentation, and self-service. Many times we find CRM center managers wanting to have certain types of technology, but not having the budget. As the *CRM center becomes the company*, the allocation of funds to the CRM center manager for the necessary hardware and software will become a burning issue.

What has been your experience using computer integration software (CTI)?

Description of Answer	Respondents
CTI currently being installed	3.66%
CTI installed and working better than my expectations	10.98%
CTI installed and working at my expectations	26.83%
CTI installed but not working at my expectations	12.20%
CTI installation planned for next year	13.41%
CTI installation not planned due to lack of budget	18.29%
CTI was evaluated, but not needed	4.88%
I am not aware of CTI	9.75%

Source: Purdue University Research (published in CCNews Dec. 2001)

Figure 5.12. Purdue University research on CTI

Self-service

Self-service is a growing area and when well done, can be a great channel for providing an excellent customer experience. If this channel is poorly done, it results in either lost customers or increased agent calls. The self-service environment can manage the customers' experiences and help them receive the most effective service. Providing effective self-service requires a comprehensive knowledge environment that includes FAQs, structured knowledge, the ability to do aggregate searches, and the ability to be escalated to assisted service when needed. Here are some pointers to think about when considering self-service:

- For common, simple inquiries, the customer can receive a rapid response for quick satisfaction. These inquiries can be satisfied with FAQ-style knowledge bases.

- For common, complex inquiries, the customer can be guided to the answer through diagnostic cases to ensure they get the correct answer. These inquiries require a structured knowledge base.

- If the customer's inquiry is uncommon, the solution to their inquiry will not likely be part of the self-service environment. These inquiries will need the aid of an agent to help find the answer.

Prior to escalating a customer with an uncommon inquiry to assisted service, they can be offered a chance to be helped through an intelligent search of all accessible documents. The intelligent search provides aggregate access to unstructured information. If the customer can't find their answer, or if they want to receive assisted service at any time, they can be escalated to their choice of service channel, including e-mail, online assistance, or phone. When they are escalated, all information that was learned about them in the self-service environment can be passed along to the agent so they don't have to repeat this information.

Self-service Web-based Solution

Companies often want to use cost-effective solutions to meet high customer expectations through the Internet. A customer service portal can be provided so customers know where they can get service 24 hours a day, 7 days a week. This portal enables customers to find answers to their questions and to have their issues escalated to assisted-service when needed.

In our research on this particular touchpoint we wanted to know how effective and efficient self-service really is. Because we are frequently asked questions about customer interaction management by industry practitioners, vendors/suppliers, consultants, news reporters, and stock analysts, we created a survey program that allows us to poll thousands of our members in the International Benchmarking Community. We think you will find the research fascinating. We asked the following about their Web sites:

- Which of the following three popular channels for customer contact are fully integrated at your CRM center? For instance, does the agent know that the caller sent an e-mail three days prior to the telephone call?

- What type of online support do you now provide at your Web site?

- Tell me about your experience with the following Web center technology: click-to-talk button in e-mails or a Web site page that allows online customers to talk over the Internet to your agents instantly.

96

The responses (figures 5.13 a-c) showed that 23% have integrated e-mail, telephone, and a Web site. Approximately one year ago, our community responded to this same question with a cumulative answer of less than 5%. E-mail was the most common alternate channel for customer communication (89%), then an 800 number (74%), and snail mail (70%) followed. Click-to-talk is a specific form of channel integration that can be placed in either an e-mail or on a Web site at strategic locations. This approach allows voice communications over the Internet. Only 2% of the respondents indicated that they have already installed this technology. An additional 15% said they plan to install the technology in the next year, and 23% were considering it. This agent-assisted customer touchpoint is becoming very popular.

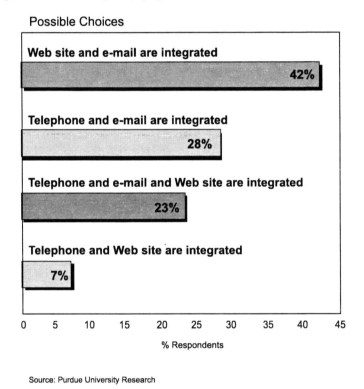

Possible Choices

Web site and e-mail are integrated — 42%

Telephone and e-mail are integrated — 28%

Telephone and e-mail and Web site are integrated — 23%

Telephone and Web site are integrated — 7%

% Respondents

Source: Purdue University Research

Figure 5.13a. Which of the following three channels for customer contact are fully integrated at your contact center?

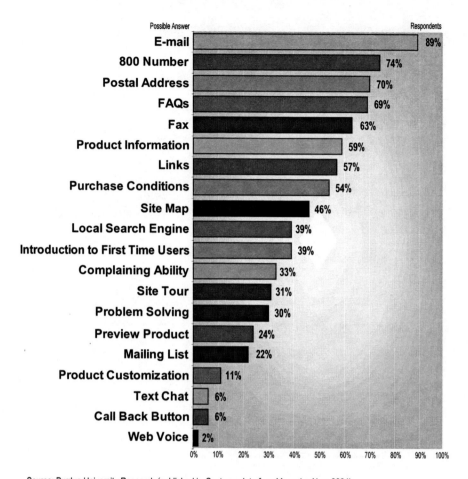

Possible Answer | Respondents

E-mail	89%
800 Number	74%
Postal Address	70%
FAQs	69%
Fax	63%
Product Information	59%
Links	57%
Purchase Conditions	54%
Site Map	46%
Local Search Engine	39%
Introduction to First Time Users	39%
Complaining Ability	33%
Site Tour	31%
Problem Solving	30%
Preview Product	24%
Mailing List	22%
Product Customization	11%
Text Chat	6%
Call Back Button	6%
Web Voice	2%

Source: Purdue University Research (published in *Customer Interface Magazine* Nov. 2001)

Figure 5.13b. What type of online support do you now provide at your Web site?

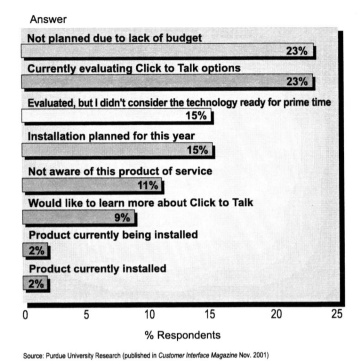

Answer

Not planned due to lack of budget	23%
Currently evaluating Click to Talk options	23%
Evaluated, but I didn't consider the technology ready for prime time	15%
Installation planned for this year	15%
Not aware of this product of service	11%
Would like to learn more about Click to Talk	9%
Product currently being installed	2%
Product currently installed	2%

% Respondents

Source: Purdue University Research (published in *Customer Interface Magazine* Nov. 2001)

Figure 5.13c. What has been your experience with the following Web center technology, specifically on Click-to-Talk buttons placed in e-mail or Web site pages?

When we looked at VoIP (voice over Internet protocol) use (see figure 5.14), we found that 28.3% of CRM center managers were not even aware of VoIP. Of those who had installed it, 1% felt that it was working better than their expectations.

99

Description of Answer	Respondents
VoIP currently being installed	4.71%
VoIP installed and working better than my expectations	1.00%
VoIP installed and working at my expectations	3.53%
VoIP installed but not working at my expectations	1.18%
VoIP installation planned for next year	16.47%
VoIP installation not planned due to lack of budget	20.00%
VoIP was evaluated, but not needed	25.88%
I am not aware of VoIP	28.23%

Source: Purdue University Research (published in *CCNews* Dec. 2001)

Figure 5.14. What has been your experience using voice over Internet protocol (VoIP)?

Here are some options to consider when choosing your self-service Web-based solution:

- A virtual assistant "NetSage," can be deployed to manage the customer's experience at the Web site and customer service portal, ensuring that the visit is a success.

- The virtual assistant will qualify the customer's inquiry to determine how best to help them out. All interactions are in natural language so customers can communicate in the most comfortable manner.

- For simple inquiries, the virtual assistant can deliver an immediate response to the customer—either in its dialog window or by pushing a Web page that contains the answer.

- Customers who have complex issues can be helped using diagnostic cases that guide the customer to the appropriate answer.

- Dynamically generated FAQs are also available to customers so they can see answers to questions they will likely have in the future and so that they can avoid having to call in at a later time for help.

- The self-service environment provides selective access to existing knowledge sources so that customers only have access to documents that are approved for them to view.

- Customers can freely flow from self-service to assisted-service and vice-versa. With intelligent escalation, agents have access to what was learned in the self-service environment, and the self-service environment can leverage what is learned through assisted-service.

While we feel very strongly about the validity of using the Internet as a communication channel with your customers, we again caution the use of the Internet unless certain criteria have been established and properly planned and budgeted for. Self-service, when done properly, can be the lowest-cost service channel, since the effort used to create the content is leveraged across an unlimited number of customers. Here's why:

- **Call reduction (call avoidance)**—Customers can be redirected to the Web site in order to serve themselves, resulting in fewer calls handled by agents.

- **Agents focus on more urgent issues**—With the self-service environment taking care of less urgent issues, agents are freed up to concentrate on the urgent ones that require assisted real-time service.

- **Easily scalable**—Self-service is the only service channel that can scale indefinitely, since it doesn't require agents to be added as the number of inquiries increase.

- **Around-the-clock global service**—Customers can receive service when they need it—no need to worry about global time differences.

- **Customers are empowered**—Customers have the power to find the answers they need. In most cases, they don't need to rely on agents to get help.

- **Supports simple and complex inquiries**—The Web can support all types of customer inquiries, including complicated ones that need guided help. Many answers that are very difficult to deliver over the phone are easily deliverable over the Internet.

Online Agent-Assisted Service

Where the real benefit of the Internet is gained is when agents migrate customers to self-service through the online assisted-service solution on the Web. A well-thought-out Internet solution enables CRM center agents to invite customers they are helping on the phone to the Web site where they can continue to help them with the

101

current issue, deliver more comprehensive answers, and train them to use the self-service environment.

- While on the Web site, agents can walk customers through diagnostic cases more effectively since the customer can see the questions that are being asked while they jointly fill in the answers with the agent.

- And while online, the agent can show the customer the self-service environment, train them to use it, and even help them register so that the next time they have a question, they are ready to use it.

- Online assisted-service solutions can provide agents with the means to communicate with customers using text chat, co-browsing, and callbacks.

- Customers can receive help and be escorted on the most complex Web sites, including those that incorporate e-Commerce, personalization, and user-authentication—sources of problems for less advanced co-navigation solutions.

- Many online assisted-service solutions can support virtually all customer browsers, including early version of IE and Netscape as well as AOL and WebTV. This means customers won't be required to download multi-megabyte browser upgrades to receive online assisted-service.

- Supervisors can monitor communications and join in if their assistance is required. This helps them ensure customers are receiving the best service possible and agents are following professional etiquette standards.

For customers who are calling into the CRM center for service, multimedia capabilities make the online channel excellent for complex service communications. Agents can take full advantage of Web site and multimedia knowledge sources when helping customers. It can be especially great for training customers to take better advantage of the Web site. Customers can be easily taught to use the Web site more effectively by escorting them through the Web site. This will lead to an increased utilization of the Web site and reduce the number of repeat service calls that occur.

For customers who are visiting the Web site and requesting service, customers can receive immediate assistance. They don't need to break the context of their current visit to call in for help over the phone. In addition, there can be an increase in sales closure rate because customers can be effectively helped at the critical point of purchase. Any questions that they have when placing their order online can be answered while they are in the purchasing mood, thereby increasing the sales closure rate. This method can be highly effective for cross-selling and up-selling. While agents are answering customer questions during their purchase process, they can effectively cross-sell and up-sell them.

E-mail

If one adds e-mail to the list of customer touchpoints, then the issue of increased e-mail traffic—the need to respond in a timely matter—is important to consider. You will want a solution that proactively manages large volumes of e-mail inquiries and personalized e-mail campaigns. E-mail list and campaign management enables companies to proactively communicate important and relevant information to customers.

Agents can benefit from a centralized view of customer information and their communication history, including the campaigns they have received, resulting in a 360-degree view of the customer. In addition, agents can have access to the centralized knowledge environment so they can quickly respond to customer inquiries with the right answers. Secure messaging can be implemented in order to protect sensitive information. With secured messaging, customers view e-mails from within a secured portal environment.

In our Purdue University research we asked companies:

- How are you managing the ever-increasing volume of e-mail from customers?
- What is your average e-mail response time?
- How do you measure the quality (customer satisfaction) of your e-mail?
- What percentage of your e-mail agent's time is spent performing other tasks?
- What is the primary indicator of your e-mail agent's productivity?
- Of your e-mail agents who work other functions, how is their time spent?

The answers to these questions are given in figure 5.15 (a-f).

The conclusions about e-mail are that companies have had to install e-mail management systems and train special agents just to handle e-mail (figure 5.15a). Most e-mail agents spend time doing other things, including handling phone calls (figures 5.16b and c). When asked about how e-mail agent's productivity is measured, over 50% said it was not measured (figure 5.15d). Most e-mails are responded to within six hours (figure 5.15e). This is in spite of the fact that when we survey consumers, they are happy if their e-mails are answered within 24 hours. Regarding e-mail quality, the majority of managers seem to sample e-mails for quality (5.16f). We encourage a greater focus on ensuring that each e-mail is answered in one e-mail—"first and final"—as we already strive to do with telephone calls.

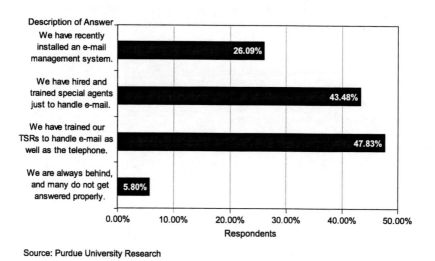

Source: Purdue University Research

Figure 5.15a. How are you managing the ever-increasing volume of e-mail from customers?

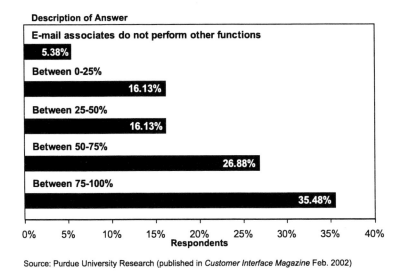

Figure 5.15b. On average, what percentage of your e-mail associates' time is spent performing some other function?

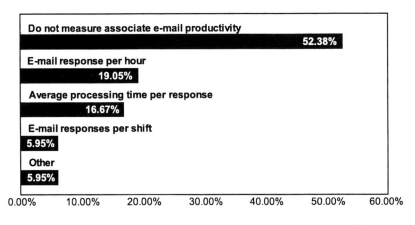

Figure 5.15c. What is the primary indicator of your e-mail associates' productivity?

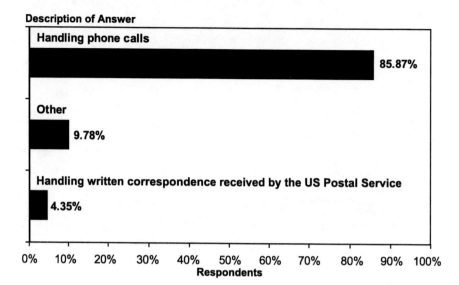

Description of Answer

Handling phone calls — 85.87%

Other — 9.78%

Handling written correspondence received by the US Postal Service — 4.35%

Respondents (0% – 100%)

Source: Purdue University Research (published in *Customer Interface Magazine* Feb. 2002)

Figure 5.15d. Of your e-mail associates who work other functions, most of their time is spent on. . .?

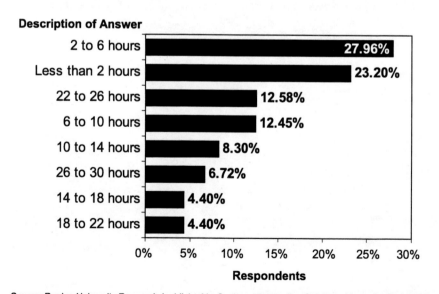

Description of Answer

- 2 to 6 hours — 27.96%
- Less than 2 hours — 23.20%
- 22 to 26 hours — 12.58%
- 6 to 10 hours — 12.45%
- 10 to 14 hours — 8.30%
- 26 to 30 hours — 6.72%
- 14 to 18 hours — 4.40%
- 18 to 22 hours — 4.40%

Respondents (0% – 30%)

Source: Purdue University Research (published in *Customer Interaction Solutions Magazine* May 2000)

Figure 5.15e. What is your average actual e-mail response time?

106

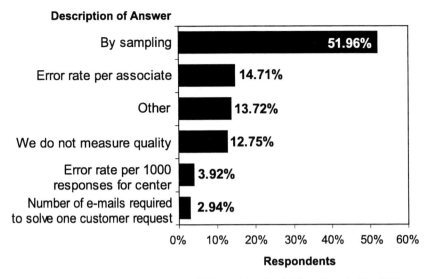

Description of Answer

Source: Purdue University Research (published in *Customer Interaction Solutions Magazine* May 2002)

Figure 5.15f. How do you measure quality?

Consider the following in the e-mail channel:

- An e-mail management solution that delivers closed loop service through integrated inbound and outbound e-mail management.

- Powerful routing rules, which are hierarchical, to ensure that e-mail can be routed accurately in complex environments.

- A single-install, multi-language solution makes it easy to set up and deliver global customer service cost-effectively.

Benefits of a well-thought-out e-mail management solution can be:

- **Increased agent productivity**—Agents are able to handle larger volumes of e-mail by reducing the time needed to understand the customer situation, find the correct answers, and create the replies.

- **E-mails responded to more quickly**—E-mails are routed to the correct agent, reducing wasteful re-routing time. Time-based routing rules enable e-mails to be automatically re-routed if agents are overloaded so customers don't have to wait as long. The agent's increased productivity reduces time needed to create and send the reply.

- **Improved accuracy of e-mail responses**—Agents have access to customer information, their cross-channel communication history, and centralized knowledge when they reply to e-mails.

- **Cost-effective global service**—E-mail is globally cost-effective since the cost of replying doesn't increase when helping international customers as it does through phone support.

- **Proactive e-mail service**—Companies can leverage service campaigns to proactively and cost-effectively deliver service to customers resulting in increased customer loyalty and leading to an increased lifetime value of the customer base.

A customer's perception of service quality is directly influenced by how positive their service experience is. In this chapter we have given you a technology roadmap. In the next chapter we'll look at how to use the analytical technology to improve customer satisfaction.

Own and Operate Versus Using a Service Provider

The challenge of today's CRM technology manager is to decide what software solutions are better owned and operated on-site at the company, and what software solutions are better accessed through an application service provider (ASP) located off-site.

Traditionally, software was always been purchased and then installed on one's own computer hardware located on-site at the company. This does give the company complete control, however it does mean hiring technical staff to support and maintain the software during its operational life. This can substantially add to the lifetime ownership cost of a software solution, and adds the burden of finding, training, and managing highly capable individuals.

Today, the availability of most CRM software solutions through off-premise ASPs offers a much different and potentially advantageous alternative. Having access to software solutions through an ASP, can be a completely different experience, and may in some cases be very cost effective. Here are some of the reasons company's are selecting the ASP approach versus the on-site approach:

1. The ASP is typically also the software developer, and therefore has ample staff with the expertise related to supporting the source code.

2. When new software releases are issued, the company using an ASP gets the benefit immediately and automatically. The company that has purchased the software must first receive the new software release, and then install it themselves, and make sure that everything is in working order.

3. Software maintenance and backup of the software is completely handled by the ASP, saving the company thousands of dollars on an annual basis.

4. Since the software is running at the ASP, the customer is relieved of hardware issues and can often insist that the ASP provide ample redundant hardware to ensure a high level of up-time.

In spite of the reasons mentioned above, many companies prefer on-site control of CRM software. Owning and operating CRM software makes even more sense when the company already has a large technical staff to support other software applications.

Outsourcing CRM Versus Operating Your Own CRM Center

The "buy versus build" decision is just as real in deciding whether to build your own CRM Center to handle customer contacts. Today there are over 2,500 teleservices companies that are well equipped to handle calls and e-mails from your customers. Typically, these teleservices providers offer the latest in CRM technology, and a staff of highly effective customer service agents to handle either calls or e-mails from demanding customers.

From Purdue University research (BenchmarkPortal.com), it was determined that approximately 16 percent of companies outsource all or part of their customer contacts to companies providing teleservices. The typical reasons given by companies for outsourcing customer contacts were the following:

1. Teleservices companies typically have the very latest CRM technology thereby enabling their customer service agents to do an excellent job.

2. Most companies that outsource do not need to be good at handling customer contacts. For instance, a manufacturer of consumer electronics does not need to invest the time and money to create a world class CRM center to deliver its products. By contrast, a catalog company that does all of its selling by telephone, e-mail, or Web site, would view handling customer contacts as a "mission critical" skill set, and

therefore is much less likely to outsource the handling of customer contacts.

3. For some companies that are strapped with too little capital, outsourcing is a perfect way to have the CRM resource immediately without allocating precious capital.

4. Outsourcing CRM contacts allows the company to negotiate the best possible deal, and to repeat this process year after year. This is impossible to do with the employees of an in-house CRM center.

5. Most teleservices companies have ample back-up facilities so that call and e-mail contacts are not neglected during an environmental disaster such as floods, fires, and the like.

6. A teleservices company can become a close partner to develop marketing campaigns. In fact, in the best outsourcing relationships, the teleservices provider acts as the customer service department of the host company.

7. Teleservices companies often offer the best available data warehousing and data mining capabilities. This can make every customer contact even that much more valuable as the informational content of the CRM contact is maximized.

8. Often the lowest cost per contact is realized by using a teleservices company for your CRM contact handling needs.

9. As a company grows, the teleservices provider can often offer more outsourcing facilities without major new investments in technology and facilities.

10. Lastly, if a company has needs for immediate CRM contact handling, such as the added load from a major marketing campaign, typical teleservices companies can respond with more contact handling capabilities in a very short time. Teleservices companies have their own key performance indicator regard speed to respond to the need for more contacts, and it is sometimes referred to "from walls to calls in 60 days."

Customer Obsession Graffiti #10

"For the staff, this technology takes the 'dross' out of their day and lets them get on with what they are good at - talking to customers. The result is greater level of productivity, less frustration for staff and better quality data."
—*Lisa O'Brien, Call Center Manager, Yellow Pages*

Customer Obsession Graffiti #11

To help with the volume at peak calling times, Home Shopping Network utilizes the services of a third-party center. Before HSN upgraded their contact center's technology, its system used simple percentages to send calls to the third party. The routing percentages could only be changed in 15-minute increments. Sometimes the percentages didn't work out. "We ended up having idle agents in our own center," explains Rod White, Vice President of Information Technology. "We wanted to keep our own agents busy first, then send calls to the third party. It would improve our efficiency and save us money in the long run."

The company wanted a reliable system that would give their customers a highly personalized experience. HSN wanted to route calls to a specific agent in the contact center so they could give customers their own personal agent.

Home Shopping Network's contact centers support television programming sales, Internet sales and other business initiatives. The HSN contact centers also balance responsibilities for outbound marketing campaigns. A solution was needed that enabled the center to integrate all of these contact center responsibilities together under a single management structure. The system needed to blend both incoming and outgoing calls as well as Internet communications to utilize agents efficiently.
—*Rod White, Vice President of Information Technology, Home Shopping Network*

111

Deciding to Collect Customer Contact Data

The end goal for CRM strategies is to create a customer-focused enterprise versus the typical company-centric organization. To become customer-centric, a company needs a foolproof system to collect, analyze, and process customer data into business intelligence. The process of creating this customer knowledge and using it to select actions that enhance desired customer behavior is known as *analytic CRM*. Note that this is a critical part of CRM technology. In fact, CRM can best be described as a process, as well as a product, as well as an overall corporate strategy. In this chapter we will focus on how to accomplish the blocks in the flow chart shown in figure 6.1 that are enclosed by the double line and are centered on the oval entitled "conduct statistical root cause analysis."

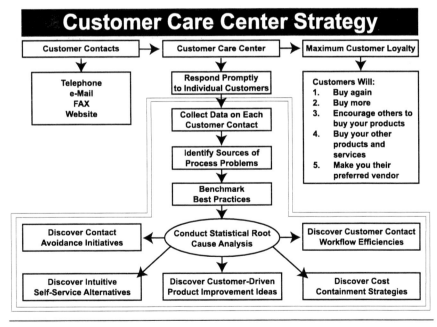

Figure 6.1. Customer care center strategy with a focus on analytics

In a CRM center, one can easily record customer contact data via the phone, e-mail, fax, and Web. Collecting customer data is the easy part, and most companies collect and store millions of data items. If the goal is to maximize customer loyalty, then the data must be analyzed and converted into business intelligence. This is the "discovery process" which yields such important information as (a) methods of call and e-mail avoidance, (b) sources of self-service, (c) customer-driven improvement initiatives, (d) cost containment strategies, and (e) workflow improvements. When this kind of business intelligence is readily available to various departments in your company, and improvements and/or changes are made, customer loyalty can be maximized resulting in customers (a) buying again, (b) buying more, (c) encouraging others to buy your products, (d) buying your other products, and finally (e) making you their preferred vendor.

In this chapter, when we refer to CRM, we are talking about it as *the process to maximize the use of data about customers,* therefore "Analytical CRM." In addition to using customer data, most companies are starting to realize that customer satisfaction information can be used to drive customer loyalty. Customer loyalty, in turn, is closely linked to customer lifetime value. In this chapter we will focus primarily on the customer data that you are already collecting via the technology in your CRM center. In chapter 7 we will explore customer satisfaction feedback data. Let's begin by seeing how we can convert customer data into business intelligence that can improve customer lifetime value and profits.

The precursor to making a large return on the investment for a CRM system is to understand the direct, financial correlations between and among:

- customer satisfaction
- customer retention
- customer lifetime value (CLV)
- company profitability.

If the customers are satisfied, they stay with you longer and continue to purchase your products. The longer customers are retained (increased CLV), the more value they provide via profits. There are two aspects that can increase the CLV of customers:

1. the customer's spending at a specific point in time, and

2. the time span during which a customer keeps spending at your company.

Customer satisfaction is the key influence (key driver) to increase these two CLV aspects. We call the financial connection of all three aspects of satisfaction, retention, and customer lifetime value the customer value chain (CVC) (see figure 6.2).

Figure 6.2. Customer value chain (CVC) enables CRM to be successful

The reason you should implement a CRM system is to have a process that creates customer knowledge, and to use it to select actions that enhance desired customer behavior that increases CLV. The CRM system process to do this is made up of decision-support software and integrated data warehouses that focus on specifically maximizing CLV. It does so by predicting customer behavior on the basis of customer data.

Customer behavior has been found to be a leading indicator of customer purchase intentions. A CRM system that focuses on customer satisfaction and CLV enables a company to make decisions that reinforce desired behavior and thereby increase purchase propensity. The knowledge that is gained about customers will allow existing customers to be retained and grown and new customers to be attracted by offering products and services that better fit their profile behavior. This means that one-to-one marketing can be put into practice. The bottom line is, if you want to increase your profits, increase your CLV, and that means collecting and using customer data.

Better Interactions Means Better Profits

Suppose you could have data at your fingertips, within minutes, to know:

- the preferences of your customers
- the products that are doing well, and
- which products or services are in trouble and why.

Suppose you could know that the changes that you are about to make to your business will have:

- won quick approval because you were able to calculate the ROI

- ample payoff

- benefits via a combination of increased revenue and expense reduction

- included strategic advantages that help you beat your competition by:
  - maximizing service delivery
  - optimizing productivity
  - increasing market share
  - avoiding unnecessary costs, and
  - streamlining bureaucracies.

Suppose you could have that information. Here's a surprise: you have it. It's just that most companies don't know where it is. Even if they do know, they are not skilled in using it to make their business more profitable.

The answer lies in the reporting functions of your CRM solution! The key (see figure 6.3) is to continuously feed the operational side of a business with strategic-level decisions. Those strategic and operational decisions must be communicated to everyone in the company. This means that customer data needs to be available to marketing, engineering, manufacturing, quality assurance—in other words, to every one in the company. Each and every employee's goals and tasks needs to map into the department goals, which then map back to the strategic goals (see figure 6.4). This process can only be viable if a structured employee performance measurement system is used along with a coaching and mentoring program to help employees see when they are missing the target.

Figure 6.3. The goal is to continuously feed the operational side of a business with the strategic level decisions.

As you read this chapter, think back to chapter 5 on technology. That chapter addressed the specific types of touchpoints. Now, when you are thinking about those technologies, think about how each of those can provide information to you about the customer. This is where the additional value of the technology comes into play. Figure 6.5 shows three touchpoints: the Web, phone, and e-mail. In each channel there is the potential to gain and retain a customer. What does the outcome look like to your team? What is the process that your company is going to use to retain that customer? Keep these thoughts in mind as you read on about creating lifetime customers by gathering customer data.

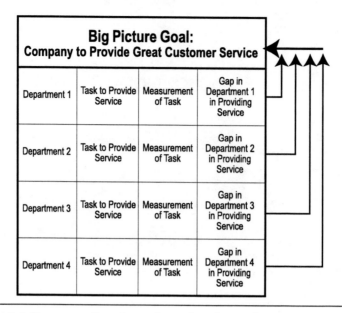

Figure 6.4. Every employee's goals and tasks need to map into the department goals, which then map back into the strategic and operational goals.

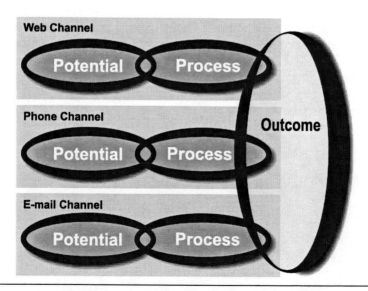

Figure 6.5. If the outcome you want from your technology and processes is to retain customers for a lifetime, what is your plan to make that happen?

Connecting Customer Data to Customer Lifetime Value

To break through the status quo and soar with the data, companies need to understand how to collect data that measures the various aspects of customer service and then do something with the information so that it impacts the bottom line.

Unfortunately, most CEOs, CFOs CIOs, COOs, and CRM center managers have traditionally used their gut instincts when faced with a customer-related decision. Even with all the financial forecasting reports, the data is not real-time; so those reports are a view of the past that can only predict a trend. And then once you know the trend, the issue becomes trying to figure out what is wrong—or right—and what to do about it. This is where most reporting misses the mark.

Many times established practices involve the lengthy assessment of various departments that might be causing a problem, the CYAing (covering your assets) by each department manager and perhaps some finger pointing. By the time all that happens, *the issue* has probably grown into a *giant problem* and a real solution remains an elusive fantasy. Worse yet, you might not know that "this" problem will be the thing that is going to make your fourth quarter profits half of what they should be. While you are trying to figure out what happened over the last three months, your customers have left you. What is worse is that gaining new customers is costing you five to six times the expense of maintaining the ones you just lost.

And, of course, you know how this story ends: heads roll, somebody gets pinned, and changes are made. And then the questions arise: "Are the changes that are being suggested really the changes that need to be done? What is the return on the investment of those changes?" If your answer is that you don't know, you are not alone.

Operationalizing Business Decisions With Data

It does not make sense to run a business by "hope" or gut or forecasting. It does make sense to run your business with real-time, actionable reports. If companies have data, it allows businesses to know whether or not they are flying into a storm. And if executives, leaders, and managers have the right data, they can self-correct nearly instantly. You can take the right action before the situation turns into an unrecoverable mess. And, as we have seen too many times, sometimes pilots make a correction that is in the opposite direction of what really needs to happen and they crash. In addition to being in the "firefighting" mode, CRM center data can take you into a proactive planning mode, so that you are truly empowering your business for the future.

In order to measure whether a CRM system is returning money to the bottom line, executives need to have a clearer understanding of the value of a customer to their company. We have found that companies generally start with CRM technology without understanding the precursors that make a CRM system successful.

Accounting Principles That Count

Traditional accounting principles focus on a company's income statement and balance sheet to keep track of the financial performance. The performance is measured by gains in corporate assets, return on equity, and the rising value of stock. Since most executives receive bonuses based on these financial scores, it makes sense that this is where the scoreboard focus remains. However, because of the highly competitive global marketplace, it is becoming recognized that the most important corporate asset, with the greatest lasting value, is the customer. *No customers* means *no business.* This very concept was experienced by the dot.com world that went into a downward financial spiral from which very few companies survived. This new paradigm in the value of the customer to the balance sheet means a change in accounting methods.

Corporations of all sizes are coming to the understanding that customer data:

- is a critical strategic weapon that results in increased market share and increased profits
- begins with the commitment of top management
- involves the entire organization
- can be quantified, measured, and tracked
- has fundamental organizational structure implications.

Too many companies, however, still rely on outdated and unreliable measures of customer data. They watch sales volumes. They listen to sales reps describe the state of mind of their customers. They track and count frequencies of complaints. They scrutinize accounts receivable aging reports, recognizing that unhappy customers pay as late as possible, if at all. While these approaches are not completely without value, they are no substitute for a valid, well-designed CRM program that includes operational and analytical aspects. It's not surprising to find that firms that formally and systematically measure customer data are market leaders.

Customer Value Chain (CVC) Strategy

The problem most executives face is exactly how to measure CLV and how to do that well. Many executives felt that by buying a CRM-technology solution, the CVC would be handled. However, with the experience the business community has had with other technology solutions (like ERP), it is becoming clearer that, without a process and knowledgeable people to make it an everyday reality, the data sits unused. Without a clear and accurate sense of (a) what needs to be measured, (b) how to collect and analyze the data, and (c) how to use the results as a strategic asset to drive business decisions the company cannot realize the potential return on their technology investments.

Successful competitors are those who recognize the fact that the CVC is a critical strategic asset that provides increased market share and profits. They don't just have an understanding of what is required; they also have financial and other resources from top management that allow employees to take the steps required to change their corporate cultures and processes. As well, they are allowed to reward employees using an appraisal system that directly acknowledges them for using the customer data to make changes to the business.

In these companies, performance evaluation is used to coach employees to repeat behavior that supports CVC, thereby creating a cultural milieu where it is natural to go the extra mile. Those rewards are based on very specific, measurable tasks that lead to enhanced customer relationship management.

With an ability to measure and calculate the customer lifetime value (CLV), companies can then focus the use of the CRM systems to optimize operations to add/increase the most important asset on the balance sheet. In the end, better customer data leads to higher CLV, which leads to increased revenue, profits, shareholder value, and growth. Therefore, adding the value of the customer to the income statement and balance sheet might be the most innovative initiative an executive can undertake.

The CVC can be examined by looking at:

- customer revenue
- customer profitability
- customer loyalty
- customer growth.

Customer Revenue

The value of a customer is realized from the revenue stream that each customer brings to a company. Many companies measure revenue per customer in order to calculate sales commissions. Order and billing systems store customer revenue information, and customer revenue reports can, in most cases, be generated.

When customers are satisfied, they don't change vendors frequently and many will stay for years. When a customer is gained or saved through a satisfying customer experience, it isn't only the revenues generated in one month or one year that make up customer revenue. Customer revenue is calculated over the long term. It takes into account the present value of the future stream of revenues generated as long as that customer remains loyal. Hence everything that can be done to enhance the long-term, end-to-end customer experience is necessary to make customer revenue an operational reality.

Customer Profitability

Analyzing customer profit means that you need to know your costs. Current accounting systems don't do a great job of measuring actual costs. Accounting systems can measure historic costs and suggest an average direct and indirect cost for a product. In addition, they can allocate a portion of corporate overhead and sales and marketing costs to a product or customer. Accounting systems typically allocate sales and general and administrative expenses (SGA expenses) across product lines. This category can account for as much as 30% of total costs including customer care. However, allocating a blanket percentage to all products doesn't give a true picture of costs.

Activity-based costing offers the ability to improve the calculation of cost and profitability data. It is based on business events (cost to place an order, deliver a product, service a customer, etc.) and correlates the event with activities and processes. The cost events are assigned to cost objects. With this type of system, it becomes easier to understand the cost of providing a service or product. However, this system still doesn't take customer loyalty into consideration.

> "The standard financial accounting model hides the value of customer loyalty."
> —Patricia B. Seybold, Customers.com

Customer Loyalty

> "The business of business is getting and keeping customers."
> —Peter Drucker

The opposite of customer loyalty is customer attrition. If we use customer attrition to account for customer loyalty, then we can begin to see the effect of the retention of loyal customers on the bottom line. From Tom Peters in *Thriving on Chaos* (Anton, 1996), we know the actual business impact of customer dissatisfaction is as follows:

- It costs 5 times more to get a new customer than retain a current one.
- 26 out of 27 customers fail to report a bad experience.
- Customers don't report a problem because they feel you won't do anything about it.
- 91% of unhappy customers won't return.
- 13% will tell 20 or more people (potentially even more with access to the Internet), further polluting your reputation.
- 82 to 95% come back if the situation is resolved properly, and especially in a timely manner.
- A well-handled problem usually breeds more loyalty than before the negative incident.

Customer dissatisfaction is expensive. Many times companies think losing a customer or two here and there means little, or that they are better off without those nitpicking, piddling, complaining customers. However, should just one customer a day (who usually spends $100 per week) stop doing business with your company, you will lose $1.9 million in annual revenues. This doesn't include the additional potential loss resulting from bad word-of-mouth from dissatisfied customers. From this information it appears that our P&L sheets need to have customer attrition added in order to

123

adequately reflect the true accounting of the most important asset in a company. A system to measure CRM effectiveness could help to determine if this is happening in your company.

Customer Growth

Although everyone hasn't figured out how to implement it, the economics of customer loyalty and retention to enable growth have become a science.

> "When you build a plant, it starts depreciating the day it opens. The well-served customer, on the other hand, is an appreciating asset."
> —McGarvey in The Big Thrill in Entrepreneur.

You can see the real magic of customer retention is when customer loyalty is increased, a beneficial customer growth "flywheel" kicks in, powered by:

- increased purchases of the existing product
- cross-purchases of your other products
- price premium due to appreciation of your added-value services
- reduced operating cost because of familiarity with your service system
- positive word-of-mouth in terms of referring other customers to your company.

Designing How to Warehouse Customer Contact Data for Later Analysis

The most effective way to enhance CLV is through a process based on decision-support software systems and integrated data warehouses or analytic CRM (Jenkins, 1999). It is focused specifically on maximizing CLV. It does this by predicting customer behavior on the basis of the customer data that is available. Behavior is a leading indicator of customer purchase intentions (Peter, 1996). CRM enables a company to select actions that reinforce desired behavior and thereby increase purchase propensity. It means that one-to-one marketing can be put into practice with CRM. Due to falling computing and telecommunication costs, CRM is now in reach of more and more companies.

Crafting the Customer Experience

To craft the customer experience we want to:

- track all interactions
- learn from the interactions
- use the knowledge gained to build better relationships.

Speed is critical. The agility needed to quickly adapt to market changes is critical. The ability to accelerate the delivery of information to the people in your company is critical.

Now we get to the more technical aspects of designing a customer knowledge system. Figure 6.6 explains the knowledge management cycle of collecting, storing, analyzing, and applying customer data and knowledge derived from it (Kurtyka, 1999).

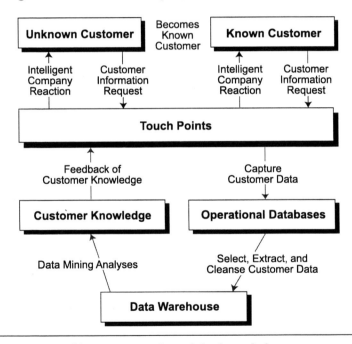

Figure 6.6. A graphic representation of the knowledge management cycle (Kurtyka, 1999)

The figure displays six entities and several processes that connect the entities. This section is structured according to this cycle. We will start by discussing where, when, and from whom to collect data: the customer-touchpoint interfaces. Next, we will discuss what data is to be collected and how it is to be stored: the touchpoints-operational

125

database interface. Populating a data warehouse from the operational databases is the next topic. Then, the data in the data warehouse is to be turned into customer knowledge: data mining. How to disseminate the customer knowledge to the touchpoints is the last item. Finally, we will discuss how the available customer knowledge can be used at the touchpoints to enhance desired customer behavior.

Customer—Touchpoints

When Jan Carlzon took over Scandinavian Airlines, he pioneered the concept of focusing his people on improving each and every contact they had with passengers (customers). He called these occurrences—when we come face-to-face or voice-to-voice with a customer—"moments-of-truth" for the company. Points where customers and companies interact are called touchpoints. At every touchpoint there is a moment-of-truth occurring.

At any point in time, companies are involved in moments-of-truth with their customers that impact their CLV. For example, someone might be viewing a company Web site for its products and be frustrated by cumbersome Web site navigation. Someone else may be talking to a call center agent and be impressed with their product knowledge and personal helpfulness.

Every moment-of-truth is an opportunity for the company to perform well and please the customer. Customer satisfaction is dependent on the way moments-of-truth are handled. Handle them badly, and the customer may decide not to purchase your product at all or the customer may decide not to return to purchase any of your products in the future. There are three points to be made about moments-of-truth in business (Anton, 2000):

1. There are countless moments-of-truth at the consumer touchpoint interfaces. Everything from product promotion to customer service can generate a moment-of-truth. At any point in time, a company is dealing with individual moments-of-truth at all levels, and it is a never-ending process.

2. Moments-of-truth can often be short-lived. The consumer who becomes frustrated with the Web site will probably very quickly leave your site and visit a competitor's site.

3. Not all moments-of-truth and touchpoints are equally important. Touchpoints that generate more moments-of-truth are obviously more important than those that generate only a few.

Ideally, every moment-of-truth at every touchpoint is captured. Implementing systems to capture data at all touchpoints is probably not realistic in a world of limited company resources. An essential first step in the pursuit of increased CLV is to identify all your touchpoints and the moments-of-truth generated at them, and develop an appreciation for their relative importance to the generating of customer knowledge. The goal should be to identify which moments-of-truth have the greatest impact on customer satisfaction and which touchpoints generate the most moments-of-truth, and then knowing how to collect via the various touchpoints (see figure 6.7).

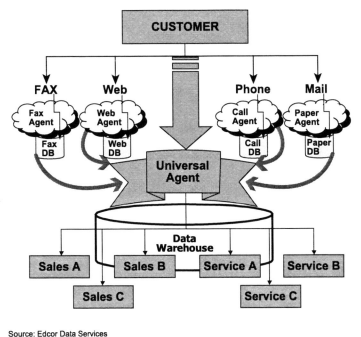

Source: Edcor Data Services

Figure 6.7. An example of how customer data is collected from various touchpoints and fed into data warehouses

As mentioned, moments-of-truth can be short-lived. This implies that there is only a short time span during which customer data can be collected and customer knowledge can be used to increase CLV. A

CRM system should, therefore, be able to capture customer data from the very beginning of the customer-touchpoint interaction. Early data collection enables early behavior predictions for the customer in that interaction. With that knowledge, a company will be able to perform those activities that solicit desired customer behavior.

Both existing customers and potential future customers access a company's touchpoints. A company has records for its existing customers; they are already known and their behavior can be predicted. However, it is likely that virtually nothing is known about a consumer who interacts at a touchpoint and is not yet an existing customer. It is imperative to collect data about this unknown potential customer in order to make predictions about his/her behavior. Already a little bit of information can often reduce the number of actions a company can choose from to induce desired customer behavior. A CRM system should thus be designed for interaction with both known and unknown (potential) customers.

Selecting the Best CRM Analytic Tools for Data Processing and Report Preparation

Touchpoints—Operational Databases

The next step in the knowledge management cycle (figure 6.7) is to capture customer data in operational databases. Operational databases are used to store data that is required to perform the operational business activities. These are databases that are used for direct storage of customer data. They play an important role in everyday operations as they are used for the numerous, simple data queries that are required to run a business. Examples are:

- retrieving an address of a specific customer
- looking up which product a specific customer bought yesterday at your Web site, or
- checking an account balance.

Before starting research, it is important to know what data is to be collected and in what format. A data collection system that has not been well thought through often does not fully capture the data needed for a specific analysis. Collecting and storing data that is never used will unnecessarily burden the data collection system. The decision about which data to store should be based on an analysis of the high-level business entities and rules (Devlin, 1999). Identified business entities and rules should be described in detail in their low-level attributes and relationships. This is to result in clearly measurable variables. Together, these variables will then be able to provide a quantification of the high-level business entities and rules, thereby creating knowledge that can be used to optimize business transactions. Two important elements in this process described above are:

1. consistency of the data, and

2. how the data are handled throughout the company.

These issues are addressed by the term: meta data. A common definition of meta data is that it is "any data about data" [APT (1996); Kimball (1998)]. Meta data describes the attributes of the data that are to be collected. Examples of this are:

- How will a phone number be formatted?

- Are parentheses allowed to enclose the area code?

- Who will have access to certain data in the operational databases?

- Does everyone have access or only a selected set of users?

These are the kind of questions that meta data will answer. A clear description of data attributes and handling procedures is a necessity for effective and efficient operational databases. There are basically two kinds of meta data (Kimball, 1998):

- *Front-room meta data*, which makes the query and reporting tools work smoothly at the user's end, and

- *Back-room meta data,* which guides the loading, cleaning, and extraction processes to capture and process data.

Understanding the Need for Seamless, Intuitive, and Just-in-Time Ad Hoc Queries by Line Management

Before actually starting to collect any data, meta data should be defined for the variables that have been identified on the basis of high-level business entities and rules.

Companies should collect both "closed relationship" and "open market" information (Kurtyka, 1999). Closed-relationship information refers to information that is collected during interactions between a company and its customers. It is crucial to collect information at all the touchpoints because customers base their behavior on a summation of all their experiences with a company.

Figure 6.8 shows four different customers, A-D. Typical examples of closed-relationship information that can be gathered about each of these customers are:

- customer demographics: age, gender, address, etc.
- customer psychographics: interests, attitudes, education
- customer purchase history
- post-purchase customer feedback: factual and evaluative information that a customer provides about the products and services purchased from the company
- pre-purchase information inquiries: information required by a customer before purchasing any product or services from a company
- product attribute information: technical and usage information about the company's products
- touchpoints accessed by the customer: which ones, when, and how they were navigated or used.

First let's look at the various types of customers and how we interact with them. We will find that some customers are more valuable to retain data on and to create specialized programs to reward them to enhance retention. This is where value-based routing technology really pays off.

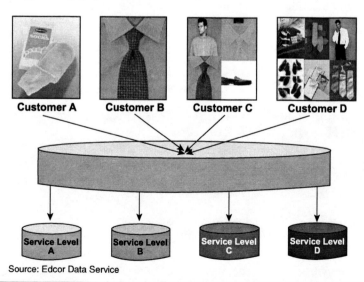

Source: Edcor Data Service

Figure 6.8. Different values and different spending patterns

130

In figure 6.8 we see Customer A, who buys socks every other month, spending about $20 each time. This customer does not buy anything else from you at this time.

Customer B just got promoted in his law firm from clerk and with this new job, needs a new wardrobe. In addition, he will be attending law school, so there will be an ongoing need to for more clothes over time when he graduates from law school and passes the bar.

Customer C is a senior manager at a consumer electronics company. She not only shops for herself, but her husband (who is also a senior manager at a car company), their five kids and her mother-in-law who lives with them and has a hobby of collecting stamps. Her teen-age boys are into music and video games and her girls like clothes and girl stuff. This customer currently spends considerably more than Customer A or Customer B.

Customer D is a CEO of a movie company in Hollywood. She is expected to be very well dressed and as a result, spending 20 to 40 times more than any of these other customers on designer clothing. She also buys very expensive gifts for her customers and her staff, as is the custom in Hollywood circles.

Each of these customers has a different value. When determining who to keep the most data on you will need to take a look at your products and services and your strategic business plan to determine if you want to:

- Up-sell and cross-sell to Customer A. If you only sell clothing, this customer might not be valuable to you. If you found out that Customer A loves camping and your store is a camping store that sells clothes, including socks, then you would want to know a lot more about this customer. You might want to up sell to him. If your store is a high-end clothing store and customer A only buys blue jeans, then you will not want to focus as much on customer A.

- Customer C buys clothing for everyone in her family. The mother-in-law, whose husband died and left her millions, loves Home Shopping Network and collecting stuff. The teen-age boys and girl have jobs so they have their own disposable income and tend to spend, as do most teens, $50 a week. *Fortune Magazine* reported in 1999 that the teenage market alone spends over $49 billion per year. There are many opportunities to entice this family to spend more with you.

But you would have to have information about them to know their preferences.

- You want to retain customers like D and offer them special promotions for things like office gifts. You might also see if you can cross-sell this person services, as their time is very limited and they will pay for the price of convenience.

- You might be a middle-level market department store and Customer B is the focus your product line suits the best. You might want to determine what this customer feels is important to them. Offering them discounts on a Tiffany diamond necklace (regularly priced at $25,000) is not only something they would not be interested in, but is also something that might offend them—offering them a special on something they can never purchase. But if you target this middle-level market buyer with the right products and services at the right price, you can rule in this market.

In addition to knowing whom to keep data on, you will also want to structure any campaigns to retain them according to how much they spend. If Customer A spends $50 a year and you give them a $10 gift certificate, they will most likely be pleased. If you gave the same $10 gift certificate to Customer D, they would be insulted. Businesses can utilize the data warehousing capabilities explored in the previous chapter to determine the appropriate level of service based on a specific customer's profile as well as creating targeted marketing campaigns.

We give these examples as a way of truly pointing out the value of determining who your customer is and then focusing your data profiling and mining to further increase their satisfaction and thus your profitability. When you can pinpoint who your platinum customers are (figure 6.9), you will then be able to focus on customers that matter the most. The platinum customers are those that provide your company with the most margin.

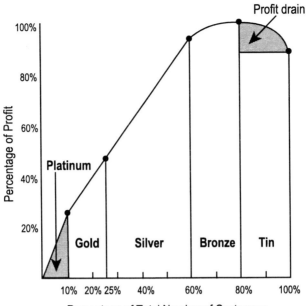

Source: Prentice Hall Anton 2001

Figure 6.9. Percentage of profit versus percentage of total number of customers

Table 6.1. Customer LTV Calculation

Customer Lifetime Value Calculations:

Average Customer Lifetime	=	9
Initial Cost	=	$900
Price of Initial Purchase	=	$5,000
Expected Yearly Additional Revenue	=	$500
Interest Rate	=	9%
Customer Lifetime Value	=	$7,098

Increasing Customer Lifetime Value Calculation:

Price of Initial Purchase of 2nd Product	=	$300
Expected Yearly Additional Revenue	=	$300
Increased Customer Lifetime Value	=	$2,099
Total Customer Lifetime Value	=	$9,196

Market Damage Approximations:

Total Customer Lifetime Value	=	$9,196
Word of Mouth Factor	=	15
Influence Rate	=	100
Lost Profits per Lost Customer	=	$10,576
Number of Complaints	=	100
Percent Complaining	=	11%
Customers Experiencing the Problem	=	909
Complaints Resolved Satisfactorily	=	65%
Market Damage	=	$9,984,353

What if...

More people learn of the problem?

Word of Mouth Factor	=	15

More people complain?

Percent Complaining	=	11%

More complaints are resolved satisfactorily?

Complaints Resolved Satisfactorily	=	65%

Customers as Corporate Assets:

Percent of Customers that Score 5	=	14%
Approximate Total Number of Customers	=	100,000
Total Customer Lifetime Value	=	$9,196
Customer Asset	=	$128,747K

Computing Customer Lifetime Value

In this section we provide some easy-to-follow formulas to calculate:

- impact of negative word of mouth
- impact of poor service
- impact of improving the service
- net value of complaint handling
- prevention of problems
- value of better accessibility of your service.

The connection between a customer satisfaction surveying program and the bottom line is the value of customers "saved" from leaving the company. In order to convert the number of saved customers to a bottom-line dollar amount, the managers need to calculate the customer lifetime value (CLV) of the target customers. Many customers change vendors frequently; others stay for years with the same firm. When a customer is gained or saved through customer service, it is not only the revenue generated in one month or one year that constitutes the value of that customer. It is the present value of the future revenue stream generated from that customer for as long as the customer remains with the company. This is the only valid measure of the worth of a customer. The means to compute the CLV are available by borrowing financial concepts and models.

For the sake of illustration we will demonstrate a customer lifetime value calculation, assuming that:

1. The stream of revenues from the customer is level across time at $25 per month or $300 per year.

2. The interest rate (opportunity cost) is the bank rate paid on the money for which no other specific use is made and will be assumed to be 9 percent.

3. The time a typical customer stays with a company is 3 years.

4. The calculation is then:

$$CLV = R \left[\frac{1 - \frac{1}{(1+i)^n}}{i} \right]$$

R = annual revenue received from a loyal customer

i = the relevant interest rate or opportunity cost of money per period;

N = the number of periods in which a customer makes purchases

In our example, the lifetime value of our typical customer is $759.39.

Calculating the value of a saved customer is identical to calculating the lifetime value. Why? Because a customer saved can be expected to stay another lifetime—everything else being equal. This argues for substantial latitude to be given to a customer contact person to do what it takes to save the customer for the company. This is especially true given the difficulty and expense of recruiting new customers. Even if the customer is simply wrong, it can be more profitable to keep that customer than to be "right "and lose the customer. (See table 6.1 for a complete calculation.)

We have found two of the most effective strategies for maximizing the value of a relationship to be:

1. developing targeted offers to stimulate incremental sales

2. launching a preferred-customer program for a company's best customer as airlines do with their frequent flyer programs.

If you would like to get a copy of the customer lifetime value spreadsheet to use in your company please log on to: <www.benchmarkportal.com/excel/myhtml.htm>.

You will be asked to input some information in order to best direct your request and then you will be directed to the customer lifetime value spreadsheet.

Customer behavior is affected not only by the closed-relationship interactions, but also by competitive offers and economic conditions (Smith, 1999). This is what is meant by "open market" (Kurtyka, 1999). A complete profile of the customer and the environment in which the customer has to make decisions is crucial to properly analyze and predict behavior, and to select actions that solicit desired customer behavior. From figure 6.7 it becomes clear that the operational databases form the foundation of the customer behavior analysis. Therefore, a company should also gather information on the open market forces. Some examples of data that could be collected are:

- market size and market share: how large is the market and how large is the company's share of that market

- competing products: which competing products and substitutes are available; what are their strengths and weaknesses in comparison to the product offered by the company, etc.

Operational Databases

The next step in the knowledge management cycle is to populate the data warehouse with data. A data warehouse can be defined as the repository for data that is to be analyzed for customer patterns and behavior. It is different from the operational databases. Operational databases are being used for simple, everyday operational data queries and analyses. The data warehouse is created to specifically serve as the basis for extensive multivariate analyses. At least two different variables are analyzed for a relationship. The more variables that are included, the more complex will be the calculations and the higher the burden that will be placed upon the systems. The data source of the data warehouse is the operational databases. The data warehouse is loaded with a data subset of the operational databases. The key subsets of data are based on the "value" of the customers involved. This is called customer value segmentation as shown in figure 6.9.

In figure 6.10 we introduce the idea of different levels of handling customers. The difference between the levels is a result of the type of technology implementation and thus the ability to track customer data and use it. We want to illustrate this concept now so that it will entice you to read on about the technical aspects of setting up the data warehouses.

So now let's look at the difference in each scenario and see how the difference in technology affects gathering customer data. Level 1 is standard contact handling. Level 2 is multi-media call center agents, and Level 3 is true customer experience management. In figure 6.11 we show the standard contact center with the standard customer touch points. In figure 6.12 with the addition of CTI, Web Chat, Campaign management, Web Callbacks, training, Web, etc., the customer can be served better and you can track more information about them. The advantages of the additional technology are:

- enhanced process consistency
- opportunity for marketing
- ability to apply the business rules and
- a centralized contact database.

In figure 6.13, representing the full customer management experience, the contact center is fully integrated with various business units or functions so that information about the customer is available to everyone in the company who interfaces with a customer. This increases the ability to track the customer feedback and use it to make business decisions. For instance, because the customer feedback via the contact center reports can be sent to manufacturing, production or marketing when there is an issue, the product can be fixed instantly. At level 3 the expectation is that strategy, benchmarking, needs analysis, impact analysis, process (re)-design, customer satisfaction and ROI are part of every day business practices. This is what you want to shoot for as you plan your technology-phased implementation.

In the last part of this chapter and chapter 7, we will look at some true-life stories where Level 3 customer experience management and customer feedback that were used to save products, improve services, and increase revenue.

Level 1
Standard Contact
Handling

Level 2
Multi media Call Center
Agents

Level 3
Customer Experience Management
Technology Hosting &
Data Warehouse

Source: Edcor Data Service

Figure 6.10. Three levels of contact handling

**Level 1.
Standard Contact Center**

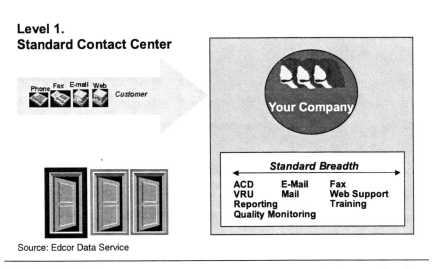

Phone Fax E-mail Web   Customer

Your Company

Standard Breadth

ACD	E-Mail	Fax
VRU	Mail	Web Support
Reporting		Training
Quality Monitoring		

Source: Edcor Data Service

*Figure 6.11. Level 1: The standard contact center with the standard
customer touch points*

139

Level 2 - Multi-media Call Center Agents
w/ Single Contact Data Management System
(customer center consolidation)

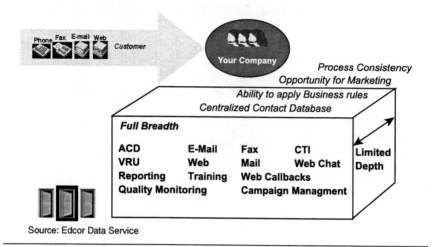

Source: Edcor Data Service

Figure 6.12. Level 2: Multi-media contact center with single contact data management system

Level 3. Full CRM Experience
Technology Hosting &
Data Management

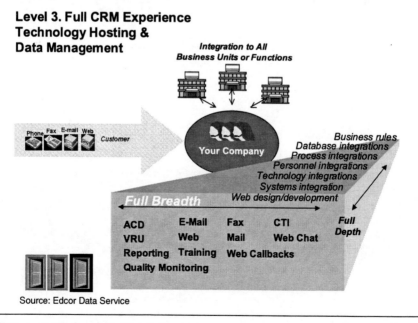

Source: Edcor Data Service

Figure 6.13. Level 3: The full customer management experience with technology hosting and data management

The Importance of Data Warehouses

Now that you see the value of the databases, let's explore some of the reasons why it is important to create another database in addition to the one collecting the information. Why create another database for data that is already stored in an existing database? Capacity requirements and date security are two solid reasons. The extensive analyses of data for behavioral patterns can be a significant burden for the information systems. This is especially true if these analyses are carried out frequently, as is being done in a company that relies extensively on CRM. Placing this burden on the operational databases will most likely result in an unreliable information system for the everyday business operations. It should be clear that this could have a significant negative impact on the operations. However, a data warehouse is not used for everyday operations. As it is completely outfitted for and geared towards these extensive analyses, business operations will not be impacted by it.

Another solid reason for the creation of a data warehouse is data integrity. It is crucial that the information backbone of the organization—the operations database—contain as few errors as possible. Analyses for behavioral patterns typically transform existing data and create new data points. Chances are likely that these activities result in operational data transformed to such an extent that they can no longer be used for operational activities. Errors are also likely to occur if new data are being added by the operational activities to the data set that is being analyzed at the same time. Operations are not being hindered by the CRM analyses if they are performed on a (partial) copy of the operational databases. The data warehouse is a copy that serves as a research database.

The need for a data warehouse should be clear now. However, the question arises whether to select the entire operational database(s) to be included in the data warehouse or just to sample it. There is not a standard answer to this question.

A traditional objection to selecting all the available data is that it will increase the costs of the CRM system significantly in comparison with a sampling approach. The system capacity needed to analyze all the data can become very large. This obviously requires higher investments. The more data that is stored, the higher will be the storage and personnel costs of maintaining the data warehouse. The larger a data warehouse is, the less the data within it is used as a percentage of the whole. Data that are residing in the data warehouse, but that are not used for analyses, are called dormant data (Inmon, 1998). Storing and maintaining this data requires investments, but at the same time it does not generate any additional knowledge that could increase the revenue. This phenomenon is also known as "the law of diminishing informational returns" (Anton, 2000). A counter argument is that during recent years the prices for computing power and storage have dropped significantly, thereby decreasing the costs of a CRM information system.

Although unnecessary, analyzing more data is likely to result in more patterns discovered in the data. Selecting a sample of the available data to be analyzed increases the risk of leaving valuable patterns undiscovered. Obviously, chances are higher that key data is omitted from the analyses. By leaving these valuable patterns undiscovered, the company foregoes a potential revenue stream. However, statisticians have found ways to mitigate the risks of sampling (Osterfelt, 1998).

Complexity of the data set is of key importance (Lloyd-Williams, 1997). If data sets are very complex, then it will not be very useful to transfer the entire set to the data warehouse. Putting hundreds of variables into the data warehouse for analyses will result in finding numerous meaningless patterns. Variables that are logically totally unrelated can appear to be related due to pure chance. The larger the number of variables included, the higher the probability of finding meaningless patterns.

Another element to consider in deciding whether to sample or include all the data is the time required to implement the decision. Mining all the data can take considerable time; sampling can usually obtain results in much less time (Osterfelt, 1998).

As mentioned, there is not one best answer to the question to select all or only parts of the available data. The best answer depends on the situation of the company (Osterfelt, 1998). The decision should be based on the trade-offs among cost increases, revenue increases, data complexity, and time to implement.

Data Warehouse—Customer Knowledge: Data Mining Analyses

Once a data warehouse has been populated with data, this data has to be transformed into customer knowledge. In order to do this, the data in the data warehouse has to be analyzed for useful behavioral patterns. This is done with data mining. Data mining is the automated analysis of large data sets to find patterns and trends that might otherwise go undiscovered (Fabris, 1998). Although data mining is capable of testing a specific hypothesis, it uses predominantly pattern-matching and other algorithms to determine the key relationships in the data (Moxon, 1996).

What kinds of customer knowledge does data mining typically generate? The most common types of knowledge are: (1) trending and summarization, (2) anticipation, (3) profiling with derived customer attributes (Huson, 1998), and (4) forensic analysis (Parsaye, 1998). We will briefly discuss these types below.

The data in the data warehouse are very detailed. Trending and summarization are used to transform this low-level data into a higher-level data that will provide the company with useful, understandable customer-knowledge indicators. The results of these kinds of analyses can be used for high-level understanding of the data in the data warehouse. Although simple in nature, it can be very helpful as a starting point for identifying useful customer behavior patterns. An example is that over time, fewer and fewer life insurance policies are being sold to middle-aged customers. This trend can be further analyzed with more extensive algorithms for its causes. Summarization and trending are useful in identifying high-level areas that need further investigation.

Anticipation is a really powerful application of data mining. This application identifies probabilities of future customer behavior. It uses extensive algorithms to differentiate among different past customer behaviors. The first step is to identify the variables that have the strongest differentiating effect on different past behaviors. If these variables were able to differentiate past behavior, they will likely be able to differentiate among future behaviors. These variables are fed into a model for future behavior predictions. This way, the company now has the knowledge to select those actions that will yield the highest CLV. An example is that a call center agent, with this knowledge at hand, can make a caller an offer based on the likelihood of that offer being accepted. This results in much more effective and efficient up- and cross-selling, thus generating more revenue.

Customer profiles provide the opportunity to segment a customer base into more homogeneous segments. These segments allow for more effective marketing campaigns by better targeting. Data mining is able to generate these profiles based on derived attributes. Lower-level customer data are formed into higher-level customer attribute concepts. On the basis of these derived attributes, more specific profiles can be identified, allowing for more effective marketing campaigns.

A last common application is forensic analysis. In every customer database there are customers who exhibit irregular or extreme behavior in comparison with other customers. Data mining is capable of identifying these situations. Often, the results of the previous three applications can be used in the forensic analysis. An example of this use is fraud detection. A customer may have made a purchase on his credit card that is not in line with his previous purchases. This could indicate a fraudulent purchase and the situation can be further investigated. Another example is to identify the most profitable customers. These customers can then be analyzed for their attributes and behavior. This knowledge can then be used to gain more of these very profitable customers.

These four applications all generate statistical and mathematical results. This means that they will not necessarily have any logical or practical value. It is very much possible that, in terabytes of data, relationships are found that indicate a particular customer behavior simply because of coincidence. To judge whether a behavior is logical or of any practical value, a person with the knowledge to interpret these results is required. If business users can adapt, refine, and interpret pure statistical results, they can get the best fit for their business needs by improving the logical and practical value of mined results (Smith, 1999). To create customer knowledge, mined results need to be integrated with business-user knowledge.

Customer Knowledge Touchpoints—Feedback of Customer Knowledge

The knowledge management cycle has now been discussed from customer contact to the creation of knowledge about customer behavior. The customer knowledge now has to be fed back to the company in order to generate revenue from it. A solid integration of the customer knowledge with the touchpoints is required. Touchpoints need to have quick and easy access to the answers to customers' business needs.

Web technology is proving the most cost-effective way to place data query, analysis, and reporting applications in the hands of large numbers of business users (Soley, 1999). This technology provides every level in the company with the tools to query, report, and analyze customer data (MacIver, 1999). This effectively empowers the agents with access to the customer knowledge they need at any time.

Web technology leverages the client-server infrastructure that is already present in most companies today. It shifts much of the PC-based tools' infrastructure from the client environment to the server (MacIver, 1999). The server is actually taking over the workload from the desktop PCs. This means that fewer licenses are required to make use of the required software, as fewer copies are needed. Obviously, a big cost reduction will be the result. This reduction in costs per user allows the company to spread the customer knowledge to more users in the company with the same financial resources. The company can become driven more than ever before by customer knowledge, which allows for one-to-one marketing and thereby increases CLV and the company's profitability.

Web technology and its client-server infrastructure also allow internal and external users to easily request required customer knowledge in a real-time mode. This way they can instantly satisfy their information needs at the customer-touchpoint interfaces. The technology allows for user customization and easy control (Soley, 1999). Customization provides users with fast, accurate access to needed information. The information that internal and external users can access can easily be controlled. This feature increases data security while at the same time providing wider information access.

Customer knowledge should be presented in a lively and customizable way. Better visualization can improve understanding and interpretation of the results throughout the company, improving the decision-making process (Javid, 1999). Visualization of the customer knowledge will improve the decision of what actions to select to stimulate desired customer behavior. Graphical representations are easier to understand than tables and words alone. Web technology is very capable of graphically displaying the customer knowledge at the user's end. It allows for each interpretation of customer knowledge and the selection of appropriate company actions in a short time span.

Web technology is an excellent tool for disseminating the customer knowledge to internal and external users. It is a cost-effective, highly customizable technology that displays customer knowledge, as a result of user-initiated queries, in a graphical format, in real time. These attributes make it a technology that can be used on an enterprise-wide scale to use customer knowledge in the interaction with customers at any touch point.

Preparing "Just-in-Time" Reports for Management Decision-making: Two Case Studies

In the following two case studies we will show you how including customer feedback in all management decisions can make the difference between retaining and losing customer and profits and losses. The reason is, "If you can't measure it," goes the old cliché, "you can't manage it." In fact, if you don't measure it, most managers seem unable to even pay attention to it. With the types of actionable, easy-to-read reports given in these two examples, you will most likely be running down to your contact to see if they can create these for you. If you show them how important the data is to the product line and that you appreciate them for being able to track this, you will make them feel like they are making a difference. And at the end of the day, that is what we all want.

Case Study #1—The Airlines

The Issue:

The call center manager at a major airline noticed a little spike in calls from passengers in weeks 9-13 of a 21-week overview of call volume.

The Unknown Danger:

What was causing this spike and what impact it might have on retaining customers and increasing revenues.

The Call to Action Opportunity:

In this case study there are a number of departments that could use this information, shown in table 6.2. The list of audiences is given and the types of reports for each audience are is provided. Each type of report takes the information collected in the call center and cuts the data in an easy-to-read format providing the missing pieces of the puzzle.

Table 6.2. Departments Interested in the Call Center Data

Report Types	Possible Audience(s)
Trending	Executive Level
Diagnostic	Marketing
Frequency	Sales
Drill Down	Public Relations
Event Driven	Call Center

This first graph of the call center data, figure 6.14, is a chart of airline passenger call volume (number of calls/day). The call center manager noticed the increase in calls in weeks 9-13. While the increase was not way above the average (the white line in the graph), the call center manager realized from having looked at these kinds of plots that something might be up.

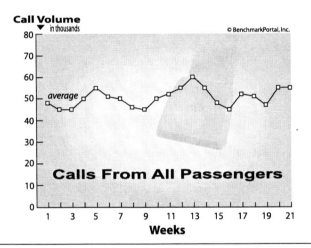

Figure 6.14. A classic chart of airline passenger call volume (number of calls / day) versus time

The call center manager then looked at the call volume from 100k frequent flyer passengers (figure 6.15). For this particular subset of callers, the call volume had risen substantially above the average calls. The next step was to isolate why the callers were calling so much more. Figure 6.16 shows how the data was isolated just to that period from weeks 9 to 13, which we will refer to as period 2, in comparison to the time period before that, period 1.

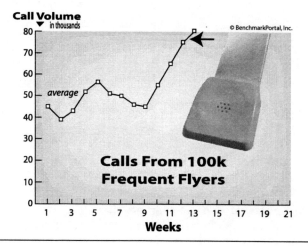

Figure 6.15. Call volume from 100k frequent flyer passengers in weeks 9 to 13

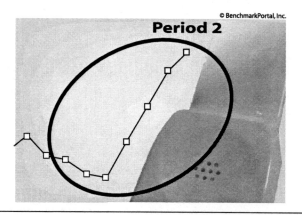

Figure 6.16. Close-up on call volume spike in 100k frequent flyers complaints during period 2

In figure 6.17, the reasons for calls during periods 1 and 2 are given and include flight plan, schedules, frequent flyer mileage, etc. What can be garnered by comparing these two graphs is that the complaints are very similar. This still, however, does not account for the spike in figure 6.16. So the next step was to look at how frequently a complaint type was made in the two periods. Figure 6.18 shows that lost mileage in period 1 was about half of what it had grown to in period 2. This was now getting down to the issue!

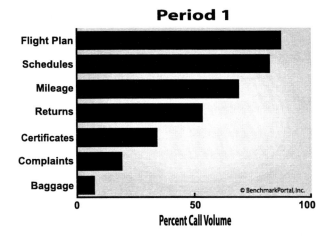

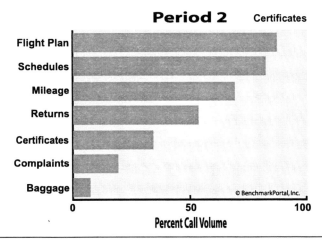

Figure 6.17. Reasons for complaint calls during period 1 and 2

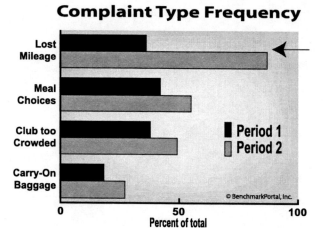

Figure 6.18. Plots complaint frequency—period 1 versus period 2

The complaint frequency in period 2 had more than doubled due to a change in the frequent flyer program, where customers had lost frequent flyer miles more than three years old. What the information in figure 6.18 shows is that the passengers were upset about the mileage they had lost. When this was investigated further in the call logs, it was found that the 100K-mileage customers felt it was unfair that the airline had decided to change the policy on accumulated frequent flyer miles when they had been promised something else.

When the program had first been introduced, there wasn't any time limit on use of the frequent flyer miles. The change in policy was telling the passengers that they now had to use the miles within a certain time period or lose them. This, of course, infuriated the 100K-mileage passengers who saw themselves as loyal customers. They had responded to the incentive to be loyal, and expected the airline to honor its word. When the data was plotted without the 100K-frequent-flyer-passengers' complaints, the curve fell very close to a normal period of complaints. This is when the call center manager and the executives knew they had isolated the main issue and needed to make a different business decision. The executives decided to create a change in policy on the frequent flyer miles. After the 100k-frequent-flyers were given back their frequent flyer miles, complaints from the 100K frequent flyers dropped dramatically during period 3.

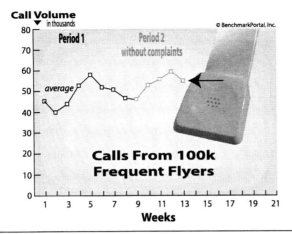

Figure 6.19. Looking back at the spike in calls from 100K-frequent flyers during period 2 and taking out the frequent flyer mileage complaints

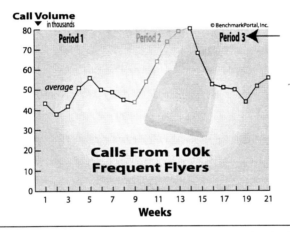

Figure 6.20. After the 100K-frequent-flyers are given back their frequent flyer miles, calls from this group drop dramatically during period 3

The Business Impact

What would make your customers loyal: having them file a class action suit against you or you providing a grandfather clause to keep their frequent flyer miles? This change in policy was causing the same issue in many of the airline companies, but only one had the business intelligence from their CRM center and acted on it. The business decision based on this CRM center data was to institute a grandfather clause on frequent flyer miles that allowed the passenger to keep all the miles they had earned up to the time of the change in policy; the new policy with the time limits of use would only be applied going forward.

For this airline, it meant saving thousands of loyal customers. For another large airline that did not have the actionable data, they not only lost customers by not changing the policy but they also had a class action suit filed against them.

Case Study #2—Consumer Electronics

The Issue:

In this case study there was a large spike in the total call volume and the consumer electronics company wanted to know why.

The Unknown Danger:

If they did not find out what caused the spike in calls for complaints, they would not know which product was not working and what was wrong with it.

The Call to Action Opportunity:

In this case the call center data showed that in January complaints jumped dramatically in comparison to previous months, as shown in figure 6.21. The next step was to normalize the complaints/units sold and compare this year to the previous 3 years (figure 6.22). This would show if there were any changes from the previous years to this year for any one particular month. What stood out was that complaints in January were nearly three times higher than the previous year, so it was not a seasonal issue. Then they decided to look at the reason for the complaints and which reason was the most common (figure 6.23). The most common complaint was product malfunction. The audiences that started to get interested in this data are given in table 6.3.

Contact Center Metrics

Description	Oct.	Nov.	Dec.	Jan.
Complaints	21.1	18.9	20.4	65.4
New Case Volume	1.764	0.55	50.09	263
Linked To Quality	779	0.22	39.57	98
Av. Time To Comp.	621	0.30	35.16	125
Reopened Volume	598	0.18	17.84	91
Av. Blocking Time	548	0.20	10.55	64
Oldest Backlog Case	484	0.22	9.01	29
Av. Queue Time	448	0.32	28.57	127
New Case Volume	418	0.42	36.85	93
Linked To Quality	397	0.06	15.82	73

©BenchmarkPortal, Inc.

Figure 6.21. Customer complaints jumped dramatically in January

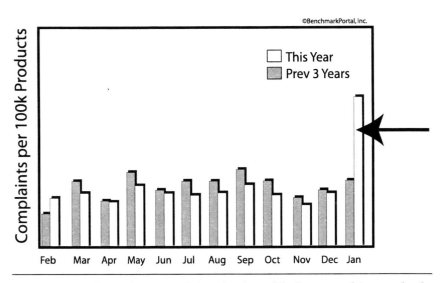

Figure 6.22. Normalize complaints/units sold. January this year had nearly three times the complaints of the previous three years.

153

Table 6.3. Departments Interested in the Call Center Data

Report Types	Audiences
Trending	Executives
Trending	Quality Assurance
Normalize	Manufacturing
Drill Down	Product Management
Diagnostic	Field Sales
Diagnostic	Engineering

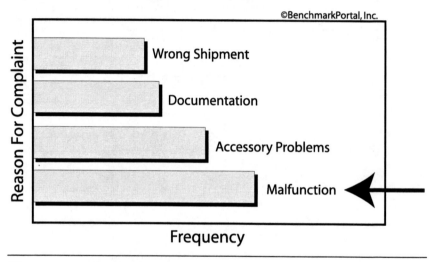

©BenchmarkPortal, Inc.

Figure 6.23. The most common complaint is product malfunction

> "Many businesses-while growing, nonetheless are often doomed to repeat past mistakes, setting themselves up for a much bigger fall in the future if they don't have a way of learning about why their customer is unhappy."
>
> —Peter Senge, founder of the Center for Organizational Learning at MIT's Sloan School of Management and Author of *The Fifth Discipline*

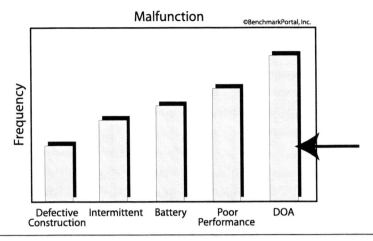

Figure 6.24. Most frequent malfunction is DOA (Dead on Arrival)

Then they looked at the most frequent malfunction (figure 6.24) and found that it was dead on arrival. The next step was to provide a breakdown of DOA complaints by product line. Figure 6.25 shows that the cell phone was the most common. A closer look at the cell phone DOA rate of the last three years showed that there was a spike in January 2000 (figure 6.26). Then they discovered that DOA rate spikes because of a new model phone: 2112-B (figure 6.27). This consumer electronics company was able to figure which product was causing a problem early enough to retain potentially lost customers.

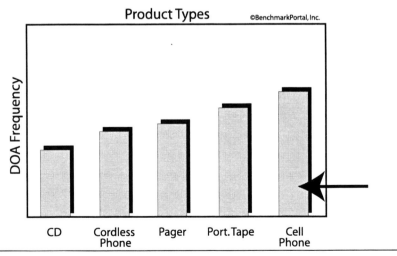

Figure 6.25. A breakdown of DOA complaints by product line, with the cell phone being the most common

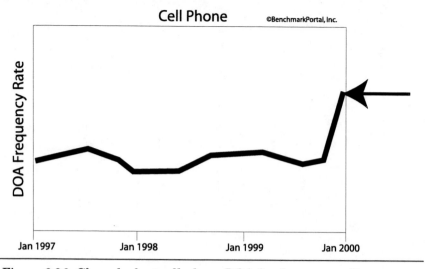

Figure 6.26. Closer look at cell phone DOA for three years. Rates spiked in Jan 2000.

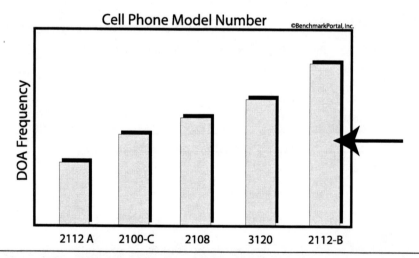

Figure 6.27. DOA rate spikes because of a new model phone: 2112-B

Analytical CRM? It is the key to managing products, services, and customers. Without the real-time, you have no idea how your business is doing. With it you are proactively managing your brand and increasing propensity to continue to sell to your loyal, most profitable customer base.

Customer Obsession Graffiti #12

"One of our key objectives of our organization is to increase the number of products per customer. We call that increasing "wallet share"... we know that a lot about our customers and can predict what they are likely to need."
—*Roger Dubois, PNC Bank*

Customer Obsession Graffiti #13

From Ed Haggerty, Program Manager, on a migration effort of his company: "The amount of effort required in moving from an installed and operating software release to the next major release of that same software is generally regarded as one of the necessary tasks (and evils) in the software arena. We faced many challenges and obstacles during a recent migration, however the real story is how teamwork, dedication, and focus can reverse a downward spiral and return an important customer to a working partnership.

One of the most important challenges facing the customer migration teams was understanding the complexities of the solution already in operation and moving the new software into place with the least disruption to their customers. The total call volume of both environments is about 700 million calls annually.

The customer's expectations weren't being met, as software was late for planned deliveries.

We soon discovered that nothing short of a total team effort on the part of both companies, along with tested patience, would be the critical elements to turning this situation around.

It was evident during the migration effort that "saying" a customer's environment is complex versus "understanding" those complexities are what turned this project around. A working partnership peaks when each company has a clear view and understanding of what is in place and what is being offered to replace it. There was gap between our knowledge of the customer's installation and the actual operating environment.

What we also learned from this customer's migration effort is that for the most complicated and daunting tasks, a singular focus can resolve virtually any problems."
—*Ed Haggerty, Program Manager, Unparalleled Teamwork*

Measuring and Managing Customer Feedback

In chapter 6 we explored customer data that is "passively" collected by each interaction with our customers, and we linked this data to performance metrics. The goal of this chapter is to begin the process of "pro-actively" listening to the "voice of the customer," and converting this to customer satisfaction data and actionable reports for management. So when we refer to CRM in this chapter, we are directing our attention to managing the customer relationship by acting on customer feedback. We provide several examples to show you how customer feedback can be used to change and improve business processes. We look at how to measure the customer's perception of each interaction, and we give real examples where using customer feedback changed products and retained customers.

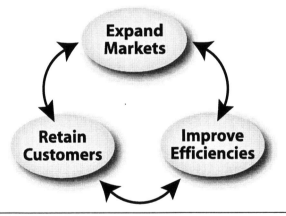

Figure 7.1. Customer lifetime value analysis

The CRM Gap

Although "customer satisfaction" is the first step in making CRM initiatives successful, it seems to remain only a buzzword in the business community. There is still an enormous gap between the stated goal of companies to increase customer satisfaction and attempts to implement customer retention goals and increase profits.

For example, an analysis by the Center for Customer-Driven Quality at Purdue University of the annual reports of all publicly owned Fortune 500 companies found there were no firms reporting actual numbers of loyal and satisfied customers. In many cases the most important asset, the customer, was often not even mentioned.

There is a serious "disconnect" between executive "talk" about customer retention, and CRM expenditures. We found that while 87% of the Fortune 500 companies listed customer satisfaction as one of their most important corporate initiatives, only 16.1% had any method to measure their customer relationship. Many of you have asked the question: "Why do customers leave?" Figure 7.2 shows that 68% of customers leave companies because of shortcomings in customer service. How can a company manage something they can't even measure? The fact is "they can't," and that is why setting in place "customer listening posts" is such an important part of the CRM journey, and the topic of this chapter.

Why do customers leave companies?

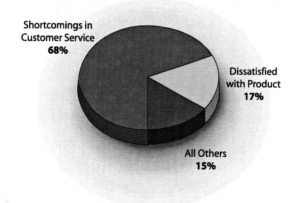

Figure 7.2. Sixty-eight percent of customers leave companies because of shortcomings in customer service.

Until recently, "customer value" has been more of a concept than a concrete set of tangible numbers. So in our research at Purdue, we wanted to get a pulse on the measurement of customer satisfaction. We asked a statistically significant sample of CRM center managers the question: "When was the last time you or someone in your center called customers to evaluate their experience with the company?" The results in figure 7.3 show that in our 2001 survey, 60% responded "yes." Just a year before, only 10% had checked in with their customers. The trend we discovered over the years was that the thought leadership has motivated the migration of centers from cost-centers to profit-centers. More and more companies are starting to pay closer attention to customer satisfaction.

When was the last time you or anyone else in your call center contacted some of your callers and asked them to evaluate their experience calling you?

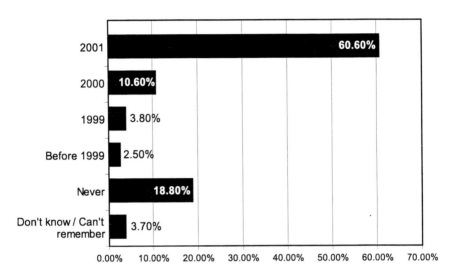

Source: Purdue University Research

Figure 7.3. In 2001, 60% of contact centers had evaluated the customer experience of their center.

If CRM managers were not surveying their customers, we wanted to know "why?" Figure 7.4 shows that 35% of the CRM center managers said they had too many other initiatives on their plate. We also note that 12% were concerned about how to make good use of the results. If customer satisfaction is so important, why are companies not measuring it? Perhaps the goals, objectives, and tasks of CRM center managers should become more caller satisfaction-centric. In other words, the first thing they should do is measure caller satisfaction, and from that, all other tasks are derived.

When CRM technology is pitched in a sales meeting, rarely is there a clause that says *one must actually use the customer data to get*

161

the business results. But our results show that if you don't use the customer feedback, you stand to lose your customers. Sadly enough, too often customer data does not get implemented in the practical day-to-day business end of things.

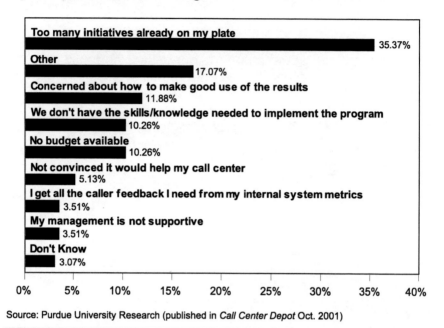

Source: Purdue University Research (published in *Call Center Depot* Oct. 2001)

Figure 7.4. Main reason callers were not asked more recently about their experience

We also wanted to know, for those that were measuring customer data, what percentage of callers gave the company a very satisfied rating (see figure 7.5). Only 50% of the callers were between very satisfied and satisfied. It is only when a customer is delighted that the investment in technology pays off in customer lifetime value.

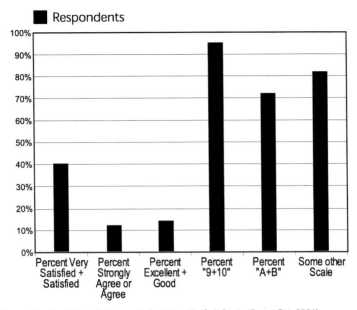

Source: Purdue University Research (published in *Call Center Depot* Oct. 2001)

Figure 7.5. Percent of the callers that were very satisfied or satisfied

Every moment of truth with a customer counts. In figure 7.6, we see three levels of customer satisfaction. Each of these levels correlates with a customer experience or perception of your company. If the experience is less than expected, the customer is dissatisfied. Figure 7.6 gives us the framework in which to place the rest of the information in this chapter.

The difference between what a customer expects and their actual experience is the "gap" (see figure 7.7). This is the gap that you want to close. Here's why you want to close it. The probability of repurchasing something increases exponentially when the customer's perception of you, as a provider of goods and/or services, increases as shown in figure 7.8.

163

Every moment-of-truth counts

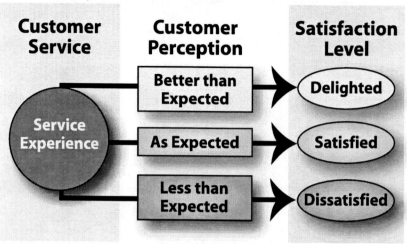

Figure 7.6. Customer service versus customer perception and satisfaction

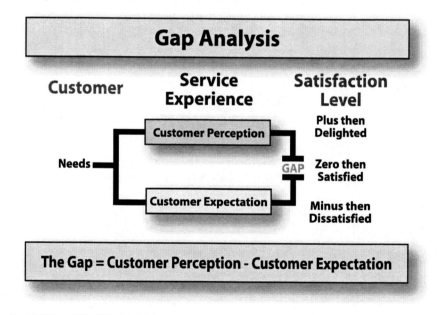

Figure 7.7. Gap analysis

In figure 7.8, we see in the upper right hand corner (often called the "top box") the zone we are aiming for: the LOYALTY ZONE.

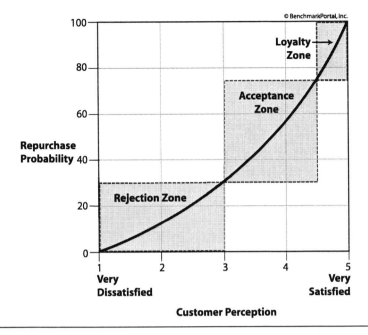

Figure 7.8. Customer perception and re-purchase probability

Figure 7.9 is the strongest proof that an effective CRM center pays for itself in retained customers with increased re-purchase probability. As you can observe, even when a product had a problem, if the problem got resolved via effective customer care, then the re-purchase probability went from 32% to 89%. This is even more than a product with no problems—amazing results. So it is not just about perfect products, it is more that the customer wants to know that if there is a problem, they will be taken care of.

Customer Situation	Re-Purchase Probability
Product with no problems	78%
Product with problems and an ineffective Customer Care Center (calls and e-mails)	32%
Product with problems and an effective Customer Care Center	89%

©BenchmarkPortal Inc./Purdue University

Figure 7.9. Customer situation and re-purchase probability

165

In the end, when we asked customers what they wanted, they responded:

"I want the right answer for me. I want the information how and when I need it."

Customer Feedback Techniques that Work for CRM

A comprehensive customer satisfaction program provides customer "listening posts" or sensors at every potential customer "point of pain." For example, highly potential customer points of pain will be found during the first few moments of new product use, e.g., just after opening the box after purchase. When this moment happens, is it clear how to reach your CRM center? Figure 7.10 illustrates how a point pain, also called a "moment of truth," can be measured. A phone call is received from a customer—this is a moment of truth, or a "MOT." During this MOT we want to be able to measure both internal and external metrics, based on what can be used to drive the results back into the company to improve profit.

The key is that the external metrics come from customer surveys, the internal metrics are derived from highly measurable performance indicators from the internal processes servicing the moment of truth. For instance, if the process servicing the MOT is the call center, then such internal metrics as average time waiting in the queue can be very important.

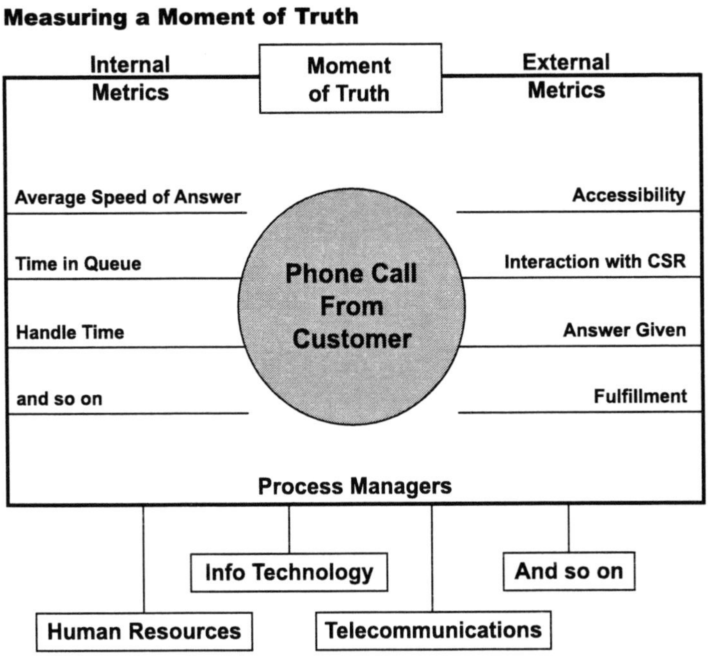

Measuring a Moment of Truth

Figure 7.10. The process of measuring a moment of truth

Internal Metrics

Let's begin with a brief discussion of what we mean by an internal metric that is "behaviorally anchored." First of all, an internal metric is an easily measured activity inside the company—for example, the time in hours that it takes to issue a price quotation to a customer or the frequency of mistakes in invoices. A behaviorally anchored metric is one where we can improve the numerical value of the performance metric by a change in employee behavior.

In the examples above, that might mean issuing the price quotation in half the normal time by changing employee priorities, or adding software or an additional printer. In the case of the invoices, a second employee could check the invoices to improve accuracy before they are sent to customers. To repeat, a behaviorally anchored metric is one where a change in employee behavior will either increase or decrease the numeric value of the metric.

Internal metrics can be things like average speed of answer or time in queue. In the electronics industry, internal metrics might include: (1) average response time for a service call, (2) the total

167

number of customers serviced in a day, and (3) the amount of time field service engineers take to arrive at the customer site.

In the insurance industry, an internal metric might be how long it takes to issue a policy after an application has been received by the home office. In an office supply store, one might link satisfaction with shipping time. An order entry department might link satisfaction to the time it takes to process and verify a customer's request. An airline might link overall satisfaction to on-time arrival. At FedEx, the goal is "zero defects" leading to 100% customer satisfaction (Davidow, 1989). Internal metrics that are closely monitored at FedEx in 24-hour intervals include late deliveries and lost packages. Failures then are weighted for their importance to customers, providing the direct tie of internal measurement to customer-perceived value measurements.

Internal metrics can be organized into those relating more to efficiency (i.e., productivity), and also those relating more to effectiveness (i.e., quality). Please see figure 7.11 for examples of this grouping. It is, of course, the goal of management to balance the two groups of metrics, providing a "balanced scorecard."

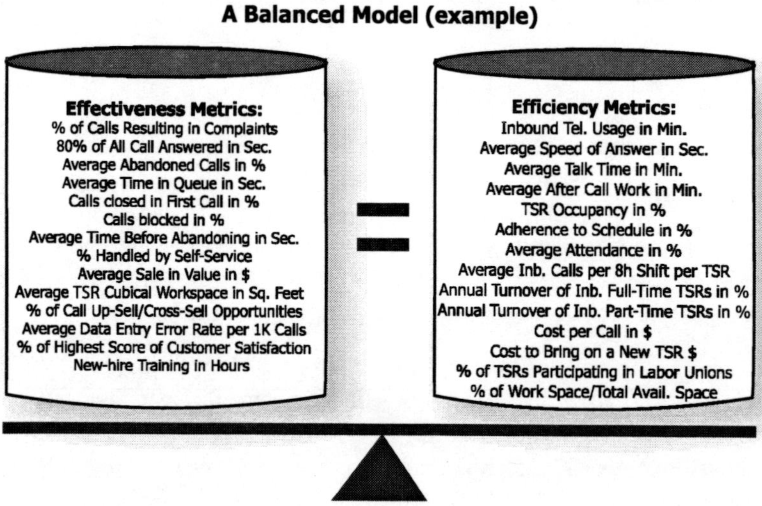

A Balanced Model (example)

Effectiveness Metrics:
% of Calls Resulting in Complaints
80% of All Call Answered in Sec.
Average Abandoned Calls in %
Average Time in Queue in Sec.
Calls closed in First Call in %
Calls blocked in %
Average Time Before Abandoning in Sec.
% Handled by Self-Service
Average Sale in Value in $
Average TSR Cubical Workspace in Sq. Feet
% of Call Up-Sell/Cross-Sell Opportunities
Average Data Entry Error Rate per 1K Calls
% of Highest Score of Customer Satisfaction
New-hire Training in Hours

Efficiency Metrics:
Inbound Tel. Usage in Min.
Average Speed of Answer in Sec.
Average Talk Time in Min.
Average After Call Work in Min.
TSR Occupancy in %
Adherence to Schedule in %
Average Attendance in %
Average Inb. Calls per 8h Shift per TSR
Annual Turnover of Inb. Full-Time TSRs in %
Annual Turnover of Inb. Part-Time TSRs in %
Cost per Call in $
Cost to Bring on a New TSR $
% of TSRs Participating in Labor Unions
% of Work Space/Total Avail. Space

Figure 7.11. Internal and external metrics

External Metrics

External metrics are things like accessibility, interaction with an agent or the answer that is provided to the customer. External metrics are those attributes that you ask the customer to rate you on a satisfaction survey. Survey results can:

- help you set benchmarks; i.e., how healthy is the organization?
- help you to set future goals; i.e., how much should we increase satisfaction by next year at this time?

There are errors in surveys, so no single survey should be used to set benchmarks metrics or to set goals that are tied to employee compensation. This is particularly true if an organization is new at using customer survey research, or if they use an untested questionnaire. Focus groups can be used to validate the results of surveys, though many times the demographics of a small group of people in a focus group might not match the opinions expressed on surveys.

Internal and external metrics should be:

- process specific, i.e., relevant to some process manager
- behaviorally actionable, within the process manager's ability to change
- trackable over time.

Connecting Internal Metrics to External Measurements

Figure 7.12. How internal and external metrics are used to improve service

Figure 7.12 illustrates the connection between a customer's perceived value of a company's products and measurable internal metrics. Sayings like "Where can I get the best value for my money?" or "That automobile is your best overall value!" are heard all the time. Value, however, is a very elusive measure that is a highly subjective judgment on the part of customers. Conformance to company specifications does not necessarily produce value as perceived by the customer. Conformance to customer needs and expectations leads directly to customer-perceived value. Companies need to become customer-centric in their thinking to accomplish customer-perceived value.

Since value is the ratio of quality to price, some companies fall prey to the "knee-jerk" reaction for increasing value, namely to decrease price. This can work as a very short-term strategy, however, it is sadly short-sighted for the long term. Unfortunately, when working with the price part of value, you have really only two choices—reduce cost and/or reduce margins. Neither alternative is that attractive in today's competitive markets; after all, you can only cut costs so far before cutting "to the bone," and who wants to keep giving up any profit margins!

Quality Perception Drivers

Let's define each of the quality perception drivers (Rust, 1994).

1. **The product usability driver** is the customer's overall impression of tangible experiences as part of a business relationship. In its simplest form, it is the car you buy at a dealership or the meal you eat at a restaurant. In its more subtle form, it is the monthly bank statement you get from a bank or the policy you get from an insurance company. Product usability is the capacity of a product or service to satisfy the essence of a customer's need, want, or expectation. For example, the automobile to most customers is really "flexible transportation," the railroad train is really "mass transportation," and the certificate of deposit is "a safe spot to put my money with a guaranteed return."

2. **The service strategy driver** is all those plans and policies you make in anticipation of the customer's arriving to purchase your product or service. In the retail business, this would include the store hours and return policies; in the consumer electronics business, this would include the product pricing, credit offerings, as well as the standard warranty period. For example, a major copier manufacturer recently added a three-year, everything-included guarantee. This fits the number one problem with copy machines, namely breakdowns.

3. **The service environment driver** is composed of all physical surroundings that facilitate the delivery of your

170

product or service. This driver encompasses three distinct elements, namely:

a. The ambient conditions—lighting, background music, temperature

b. The spatial layout—entrances, lobbies, restrooms, counters, seating arrangements

c. The signs and symbols—posters, flags, pennants, and the like.

A rather simple example of this driver might be the importance that customers of luxury automobiles place on the sound of closing the door as an indication of quality. No matter how much high-tech engineering goes under the hood, or how much comfort goes into the seats, if the doors sound "tinny," quality perception is negatively affected.

Another example would be the exciting sound of the Harley Davidson motorcycle engine when heard through its muffler. Aficionados will say, "I can tell it's a Harley from a mile away!" That's customer-perceived quality.

4. **The service delivery driver** is everything that actually happens when the service strategy is carried out by the employees. This includes the customer's perception of employee attributes such as reliability, responsiveness, product knowledge, accuracy, empathy, and the like.

Most CEOs, when they are confronted with how to improve customer relationships, focus on the "people" part, or the service delivery driver. As seen above, the customer's perception of quality comes from four very different driver categories, any one of which can diminish customer-perceived value. For example, how would you perceive the value of an airline ticket where the flight attendants treated you fantastically well, but served overdone steak with underdone potatoes, and the flight arrived 30 minutes late?

When the customer perceives the quality and the exceptional value offered, a power brand is born. Dominant market share follows. Frank Perdue, of Perdue Chicken fame, succeeded because he listened to how the customer defined "value in a chicken." According to marketing legend (Zeithaml, 1990), Perdue bought a turbine engine to blow-dry his chickens to better eliminate pinfeathers. He was making a capital investment that neither expanded capacity nor cut costs. He was simply responding to what his surveys told him was a customer-perceived value driver, that is, featherless chickens. Customers perceived greater value in buying chickens with no feathers, and Perdue gave it to them. His now-famous TV spots then focused on this product usability attribute as demanded by the consumer. Perdue taught us that not only is listening important, but using what you have learned by listening is crucial to marketing success.

Moving Beyond Perception to Internal Metrics

If we take any one of the quality perception drivers—for example, the service strategy driver—we need to better understand what business processes impact this driver. The service strategy of most companies would include such planned strategy-related items as pricing, credit, returns, and warranty, to name only a few. Next we must determine the customer's expectations when using each of these processes. Let's explore a warranty claims process. We might anticipate customer expectations to include such process attributes as minimal paperwork, no hassles, rapid payment of claim, fairness in negotiations, and so on. The last step is to connect each customer expectation to one or more behaviorally anchored internal metrics. Several examples of internal metrics that could be used to monitor and improve the customer's expectation of minimal paperwork for warranty claims; namely, the number of inquiries on how to fill out the claims form, number of submitted forms that must be resubmitted, and number of complaints about the amount of paperwork required for one claim.

Tragic to Magic Moments

In the next section we will present an overview on how and what to measure. The perception drivers are then connected to the business processes. Business processes and rules are changed to meet customer expectations and then compared to the internal metrics. In order to do something with the data that one collects, a company needs to have a customer satisfaction model similar to the one in figure 7.13, where the metrics are actionable via *a plan, do, check and act* process.

Customer Satisfaction Model

Figure 7.13. Customer satisfaction model

The primary form of return on a CRM system comes from allowing a company to better engineer the customer's experience to increase the frequency of "magic" experiences, thus leading the company to be the preferred company of choice for a long time.

We *all* know that it is very difficult for our customer service agents to provide perfect service all the time, every time. A properly functioning CRM system increases the probability for our employees to provide more "magic" moments for our customers instead of "tragic" moments. If we have customers who are not delighted, we can use that information to correct our business, learn from the interaction, and use the knowledge to win that customer over.

Basic Approaches to Measuring

Customer relationships can be measured qualitatively. Although these very important techniques will be discussed in some depth later, suffice to say that within these two categories there are two approaches to obtaining customer inputs:

1. **The planned approach.** The planned approach means that corporate initiatives to seek out both internal and external customer inputs are done on a proactive basis. This includes comment cards, surveys, focus groups, and others.

2. **The event-driven approach.** The event-driven approach means being ready to accept customer inputs when the customer reaches out to the company. This might include

173

having a toll-free number available when a customer is in trouble with your product, specifically monitoring and managing complaints, gathering information when there is a warranty claim, and the like.

Figure 7.14 shows how the customer feedback process in figure 7.13 can be made actionable. The three aspects of this process map are process management, the voice of the customer, and desired results. If the desired results are known and the current levels measured, they can be compared to the satisfaction measurement and can that can be used to impact performance.

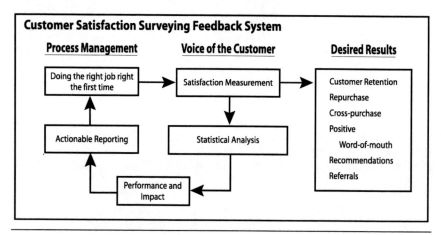

Figure 7.14. Customer satisfaction survey feedback system

Producing a Balanced Score Card

Let's discuss the example shown in figure 7.15. In this figure, we see the performance of the customer service representatives (CSRs) in delivering on the expectations of callers. We look at the customers' survey responses to "Overall, how satisfied were you with the call to our center?" against the response to the statement "The CSR was flexible." In figure 7.15, we graphed the CSR attributes to show both the call center's *performance* on each as well as the *impact* on each attribute. Notice that this in-depth output gives us greater insight into the voice of the customer. At first glance, one might think that since flexibility was the lowest *performance* attribute (64%) that the call center manager might conclude that they should train the customer service agent to be more flexible—"Give the customers what they want, and be more flexible" might be the instruction.

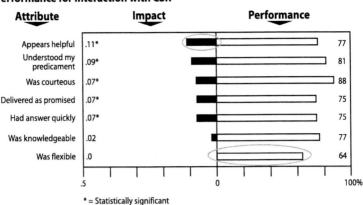

Impact vs. Performance for Interaction with CSR

Attribute	Impact	Performance
Appears helpful	.11*	77
Understood my predicament	.09*	81
Was courteous	.07*	88
Delivered as promised	.07*	75
Had answer quickly	.07*	75
Was knowledgeable	.02	77
Was flexible	.0	64

.5   0   100%

* = Statistically significant

Figure 7.15. **Impact** *versus* **Performance** *for an interaction with a customer service agent*

Before concluding that the customer service agents should work on "flexibility," we recommend that you consider the attribute with the most *impact* as the metric that needs to be monitored. If that is considered, in fact, it might cause the center's manager to focus his or her CSRs on appearing more helpful as a way of increasing caller satisfaction.

This is a simple example of "getting it right per the customers' expectations." Customer expectation measurement is a many-faceted science. Often companies try to simplify the process by doing an occasional (typically once a year) "do you still love us" survey. Because of the way the survey is designed, the results are often high scores that make the company's CEO feel good but, in fact, are pure garbage and seldom uncover opportunities for improvement.

The fact is that a company that is serious about customer relationship management must commit to a continual measurement process, much like the logic behind having an accounting system with continuous financial controls in place. Only a very irresponsible company would measure financial data once a year.

175

Management Decision Matrix

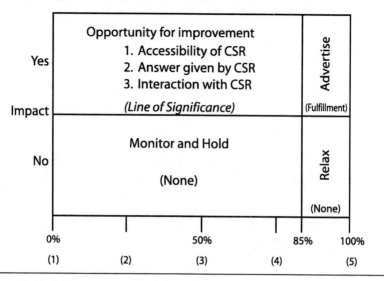

Figure 7.16. Management decision matrix

Using a Strategic Improvement Matrix

In our goal of facilitating "making hard decisions with soft metrics," how the soft results are presented can often be key to management's adoption of the results. A common complaint of customer relationship professionals is, "I present my management with all kinds of great reports, but no action is ever taken!"

One additional tool we recommend you have in your measurement toolbox, then, is what is called the "management decision matrix" (figure 7.16). Each attribute from this figure can be placed in one of the quadrants for decision-making purposes. For example, "CSR was flexible" would be in the lower, left corner and therefore not targeted for improvement. The problem with figure 7.16 is how to decide what is high/low performance and/or low/high impact. Where are the boundary lines? How do you decide the ones that are not obvious? For example, where would you place "CSR was courteous"?

In order to give some definition of the boundary conditions, we developed the decision matrix in figure 7.16 specifically for customer performance/impact data. Here is how it works: the vertical axis (Impact) is divided into "yes" and "no," with the dividing line being simply whether the attribute's performance is having a significant impact on overall customer satisfaction. For example, "CSR understood my predicament" would be above the line, or in the "yes" zone.

The horizontal axis is divided at 85 percent (4.45 on the typical 5-point Likert scale). The reason for selecting 4.45 comes from the study (Freedman, 1993) that shows that loyalty or willingness to repurchase is almost six times greater when respondents select a score of 5 in rating company performance. Therefore, we rationalized that the top box, that is, the top right box, is an area where the customer is delighted with the performance on a statistically important attribute. We suggest that such product/service attributes should be part of the company's advertising message.

By contrast, the upper left box is for those attributes that statistically impact satisfaction, but where the company is scoring low in performance. We suggest that attributes in this box could be targeted for continuous improvement initiatives or full-scale reengineer.

Lastly, by quantitative benchmarking of your closest competitor, the decision matrix in figure 7.17 can become even more powerful. Imagine placing your competitor's performance scores for the same attributes on the same decision matrix. Your course of action becomes even more clear.

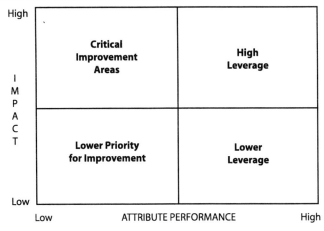

General Decision Matrix

Figure 7.17. General decision matrix

177

Customer Service—Customer or Company Centric?

Many times, the company creates improvement programs that provide the service or product from their perspective vis-à-vis those who receive and use the service or product. By measuring the customer's satisfaction experience through all touchpoints in the company, a 360° view of potential sources for change and improvement can be gained from the customer's perspective. Delighted customers can result in literally generations of repeat customers—for example, the John Deere Company likes to measure customer loyalty in terms of generations of farming families that have used its products. Repeat customers are what create large revenues with consistent profits.

Products versus Service?

What is more important: a quality product or excellent customer service? The paradigm of enhancing customer satisfaction with product quality is likely to become less and less effective. An important reason for this is the easy access to product and service information that consumers have. Internet and call centers are especially important and accessible sources for consumers to gather information about product quality. This easy access means that consumers are better informed than ever. They are able to clearly differentiate good from bad quality. This means that excellent product quality is necessary for companies to survive. As more and more companies realize this, they will strive to provide products of excellent quality. This, in turn, will decrease the effectiveness of quality as a differentiating factor between products.

This means that the CRM landscape is changing and companies need to provide direct connection to expert, personalized service and a positive customer interaction experience, value, simplicity and speed, continuity and consistency across all touchpoints. Now let's look at the various levels of handling contacts and the kind of customer experience you can provide via the technology setup. Now that you have built upon your understanding of customers, segmenting, technology, etc., it is time to put this information together to help you connect your business and technology strategy to your use of customer feedback.

178

Including Customer Feedback in all Management Decisions

Case Study: Hotel Business

The Issue:

This group wanted to understand the impact of several hotel problems on customer dissatisfaction.

The Unknown Danger:

If they did not know the major reasons for customers being unhappy, their improvement programs might be wasted on things that would not bring the most value. During meetings various people had made suggestions, but no one had the data to show that their hunches were on target.

The Call to Action Opportunity:

The various groups that were interested in this data are listed in table 7.1.

Table 7.1. Audiences for the hotel information

Report Types	Audiences
Trend	Executives
Frequency	Marketing
Diagnostic	Sales
Overlay	Operations
	Quality Assurance

They began their study by looking at the impact several hotel problems have on the likelihood of causing consumer dissatisfaction, shown in figure 7.18. Here they could see that the top three reasons for customer dissatisfaction were factors like:

- rooms not available
- lost reservations
- not enough selection of room types.

179

Problem Impact:

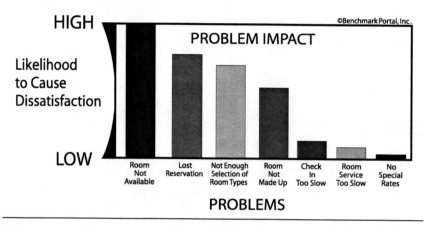

Figure 7.18. The impact several hotel problems have on the likelihood of causing consumer dissatisfaction

Problem Frequency:

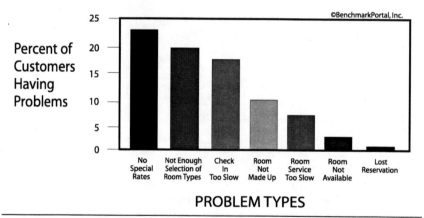

Figure 7.19. Percentage of hotel guests with various problems

What can be seen from figure 7.19 are the high ranking problem types:

- no special rates
- not enough selection of room types
- check-in too slow.

With the impact and frequency graphs overlaid, they clearly show that even though problems such as "room not available" and "lost reservation" rarely occur, they are highly likely to impact customer dissatisfaction, figure 7.20. In this case the hotel chain was able to focus on the things that mattered most.

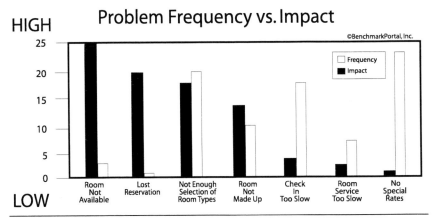

Figure 7.20. "Impact on Customer Dissatisfaction" and "Frequency of Complaints" graphs overlaid

If you think losing a customer or two here and there means little, or that you are better off without those nitpicking, piddling complaints, then consider this: If just one customer a day who usually spends $100 per week stops doing business with your company, you will lose $1.9 million in annual revenues. This does not include the additional potential loss due to bad word of mouth from dissatisfied customers. Listening to the voice of the customer is the difference between loses and profits. It's that simple. Let's take a look in the next chapter on how to gain a return on investment from your endeavor.

Customer Obsession Graffiti #14

"Through pre-launch trials, other benefits became clear—our staff loved using the new system. The diversity of online help gives staff a new buzz. It's an enjoyable tool to use."

—*John Mears, Technical Director, HelpMagic*

Customer Obsession Graffiti #15

Axtel is currently constructing the world's largest fixed wireless telephone network, as well as metropolitan fiber optic rings, using state of the art technology. From the beginning, Axtel chose to establish a virtual call center with the ability to deliver a high-level customer service, which is central to their business strategy. "We decided a CTI software solution would give us the flexibility we needed to modularly implement the functions we anticipate needing as we grow," Marco Caceres, IT Manager for Axtel's call centers.

When customer accounts become delinquent, it is high priority business to collect those funds. Now, when accounts are overdue, customers receive an automatic call and hear a prerecorded reminder message. Says Caceres, "You can image what it is costing us to keep 20 people doing these kinds of calls every month." Automation saves Axtel a lot of money and frees up their agents for other tasks.

—*Marco Caceres, IT Manager*

CHAPTER 8: CALCULATING A RETURN ON INVESTMENT (ROI) FOR CRM

What to Consider in an ROI Calculation

Executives are being challenged now more than ever to determine whether or not improvement initiatives really make a quantifiable difference. The question often asked is this: Are the new technology-enabled processes more efficient? This means: Did it result in a significant operational cost reduction? A corollary question might be: Are the new, technology-enabled processes more effective? This means: Were we able to make more money? A third and final way of asking this question would be: Did we realize a return on our investment? This, of course, means: What was the ROI?

In weighing your CRM investment you will want to consider balancing many things. On one side of the balance is the cost of the software, hardware, maintenance, and integration. On the other side are the items that can make the investment in time, money, and resources financially rewarding (see figure 8.1). These include cost containment and revenue enhancement. Then there are the benefits that really kick in when you provide better customer service. Better interactions means better business. Better business means your revenue and profitability can increase.

Remember our Magic Squares? There was a precursor to the nine squares. That precursor was your business strategy. Let's see how that business strategy can apply to ROI. If one takes a short-term view of ROI, the savings can come in the form of cost reduction. Many times this can be realized by a business strategy to reduce labor and telecom costs. From a medium-term view, your business strategy could include goals to improve profitability. This can be done by improving agent productivity, and increasing revenue through up-selling.

From a long-term point of view, the business strategy could be to reach for a customer experience that is above and beyond your competition. By providing a higher quality of service for specific customer segments, you can increase customer satisfaction and customer lifetime value. Enhancing customer lifetime value, since it is the definitive variable in increasing revenue, means you can increase profits and thus ROI. So now you see why it is so important to map your business strategy to your customer service strategy. In addition, you can also see why it is important that you know what technology will directly enhance customer satisfaction for your specific customer segments. In the end, it all comes down to whether or not the investment brings a return. If it will not, it might be best to consider not doing it.

Savings
Better Customer Service
Higher Revenue
Improved Profitability

Software Costs
Maintenance Costs
Hardware Costs
Integration Costs

Weighing Your Investment in CRM

Figure 8.1. The balancing act of costs versus improvements

A Seven-Point ROI Methodology

When calculating ROI you will need a methodology. Table 8.1 is an example of ROI step-by-step methodology to use as a guideline. The steps in this process are: benchmark, segment, target, cost, predict, measure and continuous improvement. We have dedicated whole chapters to some of these topics, so they will not be covered here.

Table 8.1. Seven-point ROI Methodology

Step One - Benchmark In this step, you get an objective measurement of the present operations and capture the key performance indicators.
Step Two - Segment This step entails segmenting metrics into strategic categories, i.e., cost reduction, cost avoidance and/or revenue generation.
Step Three - Target When targeting based on financial and strategic business objectives, you will want to prioritize select key metrics to focus on.
Step Four - Measure Compare the metrics captured in the benchmarking stage with the results.
Step Five - Predict Here, you forecast your breakeven point for the investment and estimate the total future gains.
Step Six - Cost and ROI When measuring, you add the total cost of ownership for the implementation, including professional services, support, and training. This is where the ROI calculation is made.
Step Seven - Continuous Improvement In this last step, you take the lessons learned and feed that back into the process to gain even more.

Step One – Benchmark: Benchmarking is covered in detail in chapter 9. For more information on benchmarking, we also suggest logging on to <www.BenchmarkPortal.com>. Here you will find white papers, how-to books, and other tools to help you benchmark your CRM center. Note that you will need to determine your key performance indicators (KPIs) in step one to be able to benchmark the "as is" conditions of your CRM center. We will explain more about KPIs later in this chapter.

Step Two – Segment: In this step you will want to segment the customers most important to you, and then determine the metrics that measure those particular customer segments based on your business goals, which can range from cost reduction to revenue generation. Details of step two were covered in chapters 6 and 7.

Step Three – Target: We will use a CRM center as a concrete example to help you see, in this particular case, which KPIs show a direct correlation to customer satisfaction. By measuring the KPIs that have a direct correlation to customer satisfaction, you will be able to determine if you will hit your strategic goals. You will also be able to ascertain whether an ROI is possible. Later in the chapter we will provide case studies on ROI, but here we will go into some detail on KPIs. You can find more information by logging onto <www.BenchmarkPortal.com> and downloading a white paper called "Key Performance Indicators That Drive Caller Satisfaction."

In calculating an ROI for your own initiative, you will need to determine all your KPIs and then evaluate which are the best predictors of customer satisfaction in your company. This relates back to what we were talking about in chapter 7 when we discussed internal and external metrics. KPIs are internal metrics. So, in step three we would ask ourselves two questions:

- Which CRM center KPIs correlate best to caller satisfaction?
- What is the statistical relationship of each KPI to caller satisfaction?

These questions are answered on the following pages.

Which CRM center KPIs correlate best to caller satisfaction?

The KPI most predictive of a *positive caller satisfaction* is "first time final," or "first/final" (figure 8.2). This term refers to the percentage of caller issues handled completely on the first call. This KPI measures the ability of a call center to answer a caller's question or solve a caller's problem on the first call without a transfer or callback. The key performance indicator most predictive of *negative caller satisfaction* is error rate. This is the number of input errors per 1,000 entries.

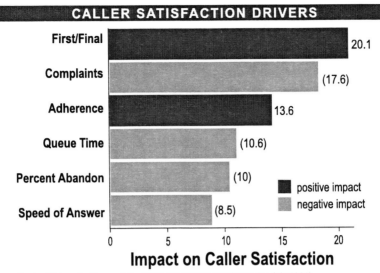

Impact on Caller Satisfaction

Source: Purdue University Research (published in *Call Center Magazine* July 2001)

Figure 8.2. The top six KPIs that drive caller satisfaction

The way this was determined was to list all KPIs that could affect caller satisfaction (table 8.2). Then each KPI was evaluated to determine which of these was the best indicator of positive and negative caller satisfaction.

What is the statistical relationship of each KPI to caller satisfaction?

This is best answered by the graph shown in Figure 8.3. This graph shows that caller satisfaction is linearly related to improvements in the KPI known as "first/final." The relationship of each KPI to caller satisfaction was further correlated, and examples are given in tables 8.3 and 8.4. For example, the KPIs that drive caller satisfaction versus the *function of the call center* are shown in table 8.3.

Another example of the KPIs that drive caller satisfaction in *various industries* is shown in table 8.4. What is important to notice here is that a KPI that drives customer satisfaction in one type of call center is not the same KPI that best measures caller satisfaction in another. This is why you cannot use another company's strategy, technology choices, or KPIs. All of this must be determined based on what your company's business strategy aims to accomplish. And this is why, when one CEO says, "We need CRM!" it does not mean the same solution will fit another company's needs. Each company has to create its own, unique solution based on the CEO's business strategy, the most important customer segments, and the plan in our Magic Squares.

Table 8.2. All KPIs That Could Affect Caller Satisfaction

KPIs for Caller Satisfaction
Percentage of first time final calls (first/final)
Percent agent turnover (turnover)
Percent abandonment (abandon)
Percent attendance (attendance)
Percent agent occupancy (occupancy)
Percent adherence to schedule (adherence)
Service level (service level)
Calls handled per 8-hour shift (calls per shift)
Base salary (base salary)
Average talk time (talk time)
Cubicle space (cubicle space)
Input errors per 1,000 records (error rate)
Ratio of supervisors to agents (ratio agent/super)
Time in queue (queue time)
Average after-call work time (after call work time)
Initial training time (training time)
Percent calls blocked (calls blocked)
Average cost to hire a new agent (new agent cost)
Cost per call (cost per call)
Hourly salary (hourly salary)
Percent complaints regarding previous call (complaints)

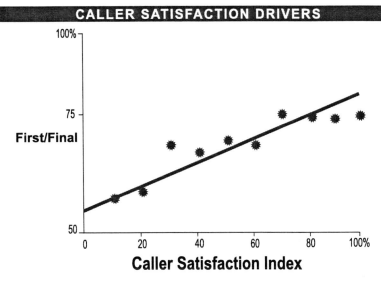

Source: Purdue University Research (published in *Call Center Magazine* July 2001)

Figure 8.3. Caller satisfaction is linearly related to improvements in the KPI known as first / final

Table 8.3. KPIs for Call Centers with Different Functions

Technical Products Call Centers:
Positive Impact on CSI
Hourly salary
Cost per call
Hiring costs
Negative Impact on CSI
Complaints
Calls blocked
Call Routing Calls Centers:
Positive Impact on CSI
Speed of answer
Hiring costs
Attendance
Ration of agents/supers
Negative Impact on CSI
Complaints

Table 8.4. The KPIs in Different Industries

Technical Products Call Centers:
Positive Impact on CSI
Training time
Hourly salary
Ratio of agents/supers
After call work time
Negative Impact
Abandon
Financial Services Call Centers:
Positive Impact on CSI
First/final
Training time
Speed of answer
Service levels
Negative Impact
Queue time
Insurance Call Centers:
Positive Impact on CSI
First/final
Training time
Adherence
Negative Impact on CSI
Calls blocked
Turnover

Step Four – Measure: In the measure step, you would compare the metrics captured in the benchmarking stage with the results of the CRM improvement initiative after a specified amount of time. This means that you have established your KPIs before benchmarking and are using those same KPIs after the implementation to measure changes over time.

In order to translate the information from KPI measurements to ROI, one needs to look at the corresponding customer satisfaction improvements. The questions to ask yourself in this step are:

1. If the CRM center KPIs are improved, what is the corresponding caller satisfaction improvement that can be expected, if any?

2. When the CRM center KPIs are improved, what is the expected ROI, if any?

These questions are answered below.

If call center KPIs are improved, what is the corresponding caller satisfaction improvement that can be expected, if any.

First, one looks at which KPIs are most relevant to what you are measuring. In this case, we are measuring the change in customer service. The three KPIs in table 8.5 were the only ones found to have a predictable relationship to incremental improvements in caller satisfaction. So these are the metrics that will be compared to determine the before-and-after results.

Table 8.5. Caller Satisfaction Range

Caller Satisfaction Index Range									
Dissatisfied									**Very Satisfied**
KPI	*10%*	*20%*	*30%*	*40%*	*50%*	*60%*	*70%*	*80%*	*90%*	*100%*
First/Final	58	59	68	64	69	68	76	74	73	74
Complaints	6	7	6	5	6	5	4	4	3	2
Abandon	7	7	9	6	6	5	5	5	5	5

Step Five – Predict: This step is where you look at the potential gains that can be made after the improvements are completed. Here you would forecast your breakeven point for the investment and estimate the total future gains.

When call center KPIs are improved, what is the expected ROI, if any?

By measuring the changes to customer service before and after a technology initiative, one can calculate the ROI.

Step Six – Cost and ROI: You will want to measure the total cost of ownership for the implementation including change management, profession services, support, and training. This is how much you are spending on the CRM technology implementation. The algorithms used to calculate the dollar value of changes in performance gaps are shown in table 8.6. The Purdue research team has developed a series of word formulas to calculate the cost savings and/or added customer lifetime value for improving all call center KPIs. You can begin to calculate the cost and resulting ROI for the improvement initiative for each KPI.

The formula for ROI is:

$$ROI = \frac{\text{Net Improvement Benefits}}{\text{Improvement Costs}}$$

$$ROI = \left(\frac{\text{Benefit of the Improvement} - \text{Cost of the Improvement}}{\text{Cost of the Improvement}} \right) \times 100$$

The benefit of the improvement is the total value of the change in performance gaps. The cost of the improvement is the total cost to implement the change for enhanced performance.

Step Seven – Continuous Improvement: You take the lessons learned and feed them back into the process to gain even more advantage by continuing to measure the most important KPIs. At this point you might also notice what else you might want to add to the system in your phased implementation for increased benefits.

Table 8.6. Word Formulas for Calculating the Value of Performance Gaps

METRICS	FORMULAS
INBOUND EFFICIENCY METRICS	
Talk time (min)	= (GAP in minutes) x (inbound calls handled) / (60 minutes per hour) x (hourly rate for a TSR in $)
After call work time (min)	= (GAP in minutes) x (inbound calls handled) / (60 minutes per hour) x (hourly rate for a TSR in $)
Calls abandoned (%)	= (GAP in %) × (inbound calls offered) × (perfect score in %) × (percent of perfect score resulting in loyalty in %) × (1 + positive word of mouth factor) × (customer lifetime value in $) × (1- % abandoned that call back immediately)
Time in queue (sec)	= (GAP in seconds) × (inbound calls offered) / (60 minutes per hour) × (costs of toll-free call in cents per minute)
Calls blocked (%)	= (GAP in %) × (inbound calls offered) × (percent of perfect score resulting in loyalty in %) × (1 + positive word of mouth factor) × (customer lifetime value in $) × (1 - % abandoned that call back immediately)
TSR occupancy (%)	= (GAP in %) × (number of FTE hours per year) × (hourly rate for a TSR in $)
Time before abandoning (sec)	= (GAP in seconds) / (Industry average time before abandoning) × (calls abandoned in %) × (inbound calls offered) × (perfect score in %) × (percent of perfect score resulting in loyalty) × (1 + positive word of mouth factor) × (customer lifetime value) × (1- % abandoned that call back immediately)
Adherence to schedule (%)	= (Gap in %) × (TSR occupancy in %) × (number of FTE hours per year) × (hourly rate for a TSR in $)
Calls per 8-hr shift per TSR	=(GAP) × (5 days a week) × (52 weeks per year) × (talk time in minutes) + (after call work time in minutes) / (60 minutes per hour) × (hourly rate for a TSR in $)
Data entry error per thousand inputs	= (GAP) / (10 to convert to percent) × (inbound calls handled) × (percent of calls that require data entry in %) × (time it takes to correct one data entry error in minutes) / (60 minutes per hour) × (hourly rate for a TSR in $)

193

METRICS	FORMULAS
HUMAN RESOURCE EFFICIENCY METRICS	
Turnover of part-time TSRs (%)	= (GAP in %) × (number of part-time TSRs) × (Cost to bring on a new TSR in $)
Turnover of full-time TSRs (%)	= (GAP) × (number of full-time TSRs) × (Cost to bring on a new TSR in $)
Initial training period (hours)	= (GAP in hours) × ((number of part-time TSRs) × (turnover in part-time TSRs in %) + (number of full-time TSRs) × (turnover in full-time TSRs in %)) × (hourly rate for a TSR in $)
Attendance (%)	= (GAP in %) × (number of FTE hours per year) × (hourly rate for a TSR in $) + (GAP in %) × (calls abandoned) × (inbound calls offered) × (perfect score in %) × (percent of perfect score resulting in loyalty in %) × (1+positive word of mouth factor) × (customer lifetime value in $) × (1 - percent abandoned that call back in %)
Costs to recruit a new TSR ($)	= (GAP in $) × ((number of part-time TSRs × (turnover of part-time TSRs in %) + (number of full-time TSRs) × (turnover in full-time TSRs in %))
Hourly rate for a TSR ($)	= (GAP in $) × (number of FTE hours per year)
INBOUND EFFECTIVENESS METRICS	
Up- and cross-sell opportunities (%)	= (GAP in %) × (IF up- & cross-sell opportunities that result in sale in % = 0 THEN take industry average ELSE take up- & cross-sell opportunities that result in sale in %) × (inbound calls handled) × (average sales value per call in $))
Up- and cross-sell resulting in a sale (%)	= (GAP in %) ×(IF up- & cross-sell opportunities in % = 0 THEN take industry average ELSE take up- & cross-sell opportunities in %) × (inbound calls handled) × (average sales value per call in $))
Perfect caller satisfaction score (%)	= (GAP in %) × (inbound calls handled) × (percent of perfect score resulting in loyalty in %) × (1 + positive word of mouth factor) × (customer lifetime value in $)
Once and done, or first time final calls (%)	= (GAP in %) × (inbound calls handled) × (talk time in minutes) + (after call work time in minutes) / (60 minutes in an hour) × (hourly rate of a TSR in $) + (GAP in %) × (inbound calls handled) × (percent of perfect score resulting in loyalty in %) × (1 + positive word of mouth factor) × (customer lifetime value in $)

194

Examples of How CRM Solutions Can Be Self-funding

Case Study #1

This is an example of a CRM technology implementation that resulted in improved performance. The financial institution, a bank holding company, is a national specialty housing finance company that provides a variety of financial services, including the financing of manufactured housing. A significant percentage of this company's customers are sub-prime borrowers, meaning less-than-creditworthy customers.

In the spring of 2000, the regional manager of the financial institution's collections call center received executive approval to centralize the collection of 10- to 29-day delinquent accounts for the manufactured housing loan portfolio in a single collection center in Ontario, California. At that time, collections were handled in 40 branch offices across the country. Delinquencies were climbing. The company acknowledged the importance of connecting with their borrowers by the time their account reached 15 days past due. However, prior to consolidation, the call center was not meeting this goal.

The regional manager realized that for the new call center to be truly effective, the company needed to consolidate its collections operations, and implement a predictive dialing system to improve outbound calling efficiency (hereafter this may at times be referred to as the "improvement initiative"). After considering several alternative suppliers of predictive dialers, the CRM team selected an outbound call management system to do the job. This was the regional manager's first experience with predictive dialing technology. In spite of the fact that he was very aware of the "sweat shop" image evoked when one thinks of collections centers using dialers, he was determined to build a collections center with motivated, productive, professional collection agents and managers. The change in technology would be one of many steps he would take to create this new reality.

The predictive dialer product includes predictive outbound dialing, blended inbound/outbound call management, reliable case tracking, and sophisticated call and case status reporting. The product focuses on the call center management processes related primarily to outbound telemarketing, telesales, tele-research, and tele-collections. For this case study, we focus primarily on the

195

outbound collection function and the use of the predictive dialer features of the product.

Step One - Benchmark

Prior to the change, this company performed all past due collections functions on a distributed basis, with its collections agents residing in one of 40 branch offices around the country. The agents were responsible for collections of all delinquent accounts from 15 days past due to final resolution. Management was decentralized and accountability was vague.

The collection agents manually dialed each delinquent account. It took an average of 63 seconds of agent time for every telephone number dialed. The activities and the average time required to perform each activity (figure 8.4) were as follows:

- Reviewing the account information took, on average, 15 seconds per call.

- Dialing the number took, on average, 4 seconds average per call.

- Waiting for the call to be answered or ring enough times to determine that no one would answer took, on average, 20 seconds per call.

- Leaving a message, if an automatic answering machine answered the call, took, on average, 20 seconds per call on approximately 20% of all dials attempted. This computes to an average 4 seconds of per call placed.

- Performing unaccounted-for activities between calls took, on average, 20 seconds per call.

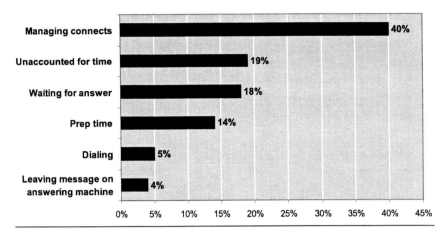

Figure 8.4. Percent time spent per agent-hour

Step Two - Segment

This company's strategic business goals were to reduce costs and increase productivity. In particular, they wanted to:

- stabilize hours of operation
- reduce annual turnover
- increase agent retention, i.e., average time employed as a collections professional
- standardize recruiting, screening, training, monitoring, and coaching practices
- create a team of collections professionals who:
  - understand their products and customers, and the regional differences that exist between customers
  - understand exactly what is expected of them
  - work as a team.

Step Three - Target

Agents spent almost 35 minutes out of every hour worked trying to reach a real person, which is the first step toward realizing a promise to pay, and only 25 minutes working with a "live customer" on delinquent accounts following a connect. Obviously, the interaction with live customers is what produces successful collections. These are the KPIs they wanted to improve:

- dials per agent-hour
- leaving messages on automatic answering machines per agent-hour
- connects per agent-hour
- promises to pay per agent-hour.

Step 4 - Measure

AFTER consolidation of the 15- to 29-day delinquent collections effort and implementation of predictive dialer product, the following process steps were typical. They felt they were going to be able to break even quickly, because the delinquent accounts (over 15 days due) are automatically identified by the new predictive dialer. A call is placed to the number identified by the predictive dialer for the delinquent account. Time passes while waiting for the call to be answered. After a certain number of rings (between 4 and 6) with no answer, the call is abandoned. If an automatic answering machine answers the call, a message is left. In either of these cases, if the predictive dialer has an alternate number on file for the borrower, that number will then be dialed immediately.

When a real individual answers, the call is instantly connected to the next available collection agent and a "connect" occurs. The agent then determines if the individual on the telephone is the customer (borrower) on the delinquent loan document and, therefore, responsible for payment. If not, the agent will determine the best way to reach the loan holder, either by leaving a message or requesting a different telephone number for the borrower. The agent then immediately dials the new number. When the agent has reached the actual loan holder, a contact has occurred. This contact may have come from an outbound call or, from an inbound call created when the loan holder calls the company as a result of a message being left from a prior collection call. Once the collections agent has a contact, he or she attempts to get a promise to pay ("PTP"), which is the ultimate goal of the collections process.

These are some of the results that were measured:

- The predictive dialer increased the number of dials attempted per agent-hour by 257% as compared to the previous manual dial process.

- With the predictive dialer in place, agents were able to handle 3.6 times more calls per agent-hour than they were in the previous manual dialing environment.

- The predictive dialer increased connects per agent-hour by 150% as compared to the previous manual dial process.

- With the predictive dialer in place, agents were able to handle 2.5 times more calls per agent-hour than they were in the manual dialing process.

- After installing the predictive dialer, customer contacts and promises to pay per agent-hour increased by 129%, as compared to results of the manual process.

- This means that the company was reaching 2.3 times more customers per agent-hour with the predictive dialer in place.

- After implementing the solution, the average agent time on the system (talk time, wrap time, and available time) increased by 9% from 6.6 to 7.2 hours per agent-day.

- The new system allowed the company to reduce, by almost 60%, their collections staff of full-time equivalents (FTEs), who were doing collections on the 15- to 29-day past-due accounts.

- The new system reduced the cost per "promise to pay" by over 60%.

Step Five - Predict

The company started to look at the change in performance with excitement and to predict the breakeven point. Here's what they found: Each day after implementing the improvement initiative, the company downloaded an average of 40,000 delinquent accounts to the predictive dialer. The dialer called each account, waited for an answer, and, if answered, sensed if it reached an answering machine or a real person. The dialer then left a message on an automatic answering machine. When an individual responded, the dialer connected the call to the next available collections agent. If there were no answer and the predictive dialer had an alternate number on file, then the dialer would go to that number and redial immediately.

Essentially, the predictive dialer performed the tasks associated with making a connect that the collections agents were performing in the manual environment. After implementing the predictive dialer, for every agent-hour worked, approximately 35 minutes were saved and could be spent working with real live customers with delinquent accounts! As a result, the company's collections agents were now able to:

- handle, on average, 32.8 connects per agent-hour
- generate 14.2 contacts per agent-hour
- obtain 10.3 promises to pay per agent-hour.

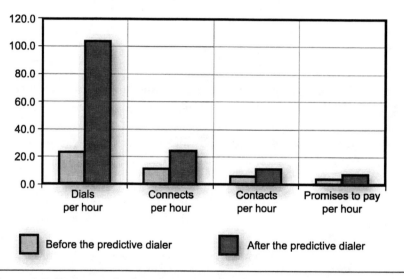

Figure 8.5. Before and after the predictive dialer

Prior to the consolidation of collections and the addition of a predictive dialer, collections agents worked in 40 different locations, reporting to 40 different managers, who were overseeing collections as well as other business functions. Uniformity and consistency of the collections operations and processes were not possible under this structure.

Today, since consolidation and implementation of the predictive dialer, the same 10- to 29-day delinquent account collections operation is managed by a single, dedicated collections manager and his staff of four supervisors. This has introduced uniformity and consistency of processes and operations into the collections process, and has eliminated the collections management burden from each of the remote sites.

In addition to the technology, the call center manager has defined clear performance goals for the collections agent staff. This was in part to rise above the "sweat shop" mentality of many collection agencies. These goals included:

1. Show up for work every day as scheduled.

2. Log on to the system and be available to handle calls 7.2 hours out of every 8-hour shift.

3. Manage each contact professionally, treating each borrower with respect while remaining focused on the ultimate goal of gaining a promise to pay.

The call center manager and his team also used the reporting, monitoring, and coaching features to measure and reinforce these goals. Prior to this, the collections managers had to wait a day or more to get agent performance data from the "home-grown" collections system. Now, they get critical data in real time, anytime.

Also, prior to the implementation, the only available method for assessing contact quality and coaching was side-by-side monitoring. Today the call center manager and his managers use the monitoring and coaching features to silently monitor calls and make real-time suggestions, heard by the agent but not the customer, during or immediately after a call.

To further reinforce their performance expectations, the call center manager developed an incentive compensation plan that uses a comprehensive picture of each agent by merging performance data from each call, along with the monitoring and coaching results, with the predicative database. By making these changes in management practices (figure 8.5) with the same number of collection agents working in a more professional, sustained, and consistent collections effort, the company has also been able to:

- improve the agents' handling of inbound calls by:
  - answering 99.5% of all inbound calls immediately
  - converting 63.5% of inbound calls into promises to pay.
- reduce 15-day delinquencies by 6%.

Step Six - Cost and ROI

The total cost to the company to create, build out, acquire the necessary technology, recruit, train, and staff their centralized collection operation was approximately $20,000 per agent position for 40 agent positions, totaling $800,000. Each position is now generating 2.3 times the number of promises to pay at an average cost that is $3.94 less than the cost of generating a promise to pay before consolidation and implementation of predicative dialer solution (figure 8.6). This equates to annual savings of $65,000 per agent position and provides the company with a stellar ROI that exceeds 200%. The company was able to realize their initial investment in four months.

The formula for ROI is:

$$ROI = \frac{\text{Net Improvement Benefits}}{\text{Improvement Costs}}$$

$$ROI = \left(\frac{\text{Benefit of the Improvement} - \text{Cost of the Improvement}}{\text{Cost of the Improvement}} \right) \times 100$$

The benefit of the improvement is the total value of the change in performance gaps which is $65,000/agent x 40 agents = $2,600,000. The cost of the improvement is the total cost to implement the change for enhanced performance = $800,000.

$$ROI = \frac{\$2,600,000 - \$800,000}{\$800,000} \times 100$$

$$ROI = \frac{\$1,800,000}{\$800,000} \times 100$$

$$ROI = 2.25 \times 100$$

$$ROI = 225\%.$$

This means that every dollar spent on the improvement it returns ~two dollars to the company. In this company there were many benefits to be realized that would mean the breakeven point would be soon after the implementation. The benefits ranged from:

- centralizing the collections function into a single call center operation

- enabling the collections process with a robust call management system that includes predictive dialing, blended inbound/outbound call management, and sophisticated reporting
- implementing proven call center management processes.

They were able to reduce headcount and turnover and reach delinquent accounts earlier in their delinquency and with greater frequency. In addition, they were able to increase the average agent time on the system per agent day worked by 10%, and more than double the number of:

- connects per agent-hour,
- contacts per agent-hour, and
- promises to pay per agent-hour
- decrease by 6% the percentage of customers becoming 15-day delinquencies
- raise the level of professionalism of the collections agents and the management team overseeing the collections center
- reduce the average cost per promise to pay by 60%
- reduce operating expenses by $65,000 per agent position per year.

Figure 8.6. The decrease in "cost per promise to pay"

Step Seven - Continuous Improvement

In this last step, you would take the lessons learned and feed them back into the process to gain even more advantage. In this case, this company used that information and improved the company even more:

- A collection agent now contacts past due accounts at least three times before they reach 29-days delinquent. Prior to installing technology, delinquent borrowers were reached only once.

- Once the collections center began operation and delinquent accounts were being called on a regular basis, customers were reporting that they were surprised they were being called, as they had not been previously contacted.

- The span of control in the decentralized environment was one manager for every five collection agents. The span of control in the centralized collections center is one manager for every ten collectors.

- Each month, managers in the collections center are required to silently monitor five calls per rep, perform side-by-side monitoring on five additional calls per rep, and audit five documentation packages in the technology per rep. Prior to centralization, the only requirement was auditing the follow-up documentation for each collector's accounts that remained delinquent at the end of the month.

- When the technology was first installed, the call center manager set the Time-on-System goal at 6.6 hours per 8-hour shift. The reports from Unison showed that agents were achieving 7.0 hours, so he raised the goal. After six months, the agents were achieving 7.2 hours, which is now the goal.

- The centralization was broken into two phases, bringing on two units each with 20 agents. It took the second unit 90 days to reach the performance level of the first unit.

Case Study #2

Background

The Australian Tax Office (ATO) is a government revenue agency serving over 3 million Australian business and professional advisors. In 1999, the ATO was facing two major business issues: one of the biggest changes to the tax system in 50 years and a need to standardize on a high-quality service to Taxpayer's Charter. Without new technology and business processes, the ATO could not hope to manage the 300% increase in inquiries that would soon follow. The organization contained 1,200 agents. Peak call volume was 627,000 inbound calls and 50,000 outbound calls per day.

Driven by these urgent needs to improve their customer service and advice operations, the ATO decided to implement a routing solution in all nine call centers nationally. In the past, calls had been handled very loosely. They had ACD functionality and a team environment. Groups of agents were required to log on to queues/ACD splits for which they had the appropriate skill sets. These teams would staff the phones for a particular service window, but it was not sufficient. The felt they needed the next generation technology, but the solution had to be running by June 1999.

The plan was to add the new technology in a phased implementation, where the basics were installed first and then functionality rolled out when they could do it. They choose a technology solution where, with this in mind, they could add technology in the future.

Step One - Benchmark

Early in 1999, a review of the ATO's call management practices found that the ATO was lagging behind the industry standard in both technology and business process via benchmarking. A decision was made to move the ATO away from the traditional public sector way of doing things and into a commercial call center environment.

Step Two - Segment

Not all the key points of improvement were focused on cost reduction, which can be unusual for a government organization. A big focus for them was to increase the businesses' compliance with the tax regulation. The more that people understood their tax obligation (they owed taxes), the more tax revenue could be collected. And they also knew if they did their job more efficiently and effectively, they would be getting fewer calls.

Step Three - Target

Apart from increased tax revenue, the ATO wanted to improve the productivity of their phone operations, consolidating the number of answering points by having nine call centers which would be fronted by a single telephone number. The existing operations could rarely answer a complex query in one attempt, leading to multiple call transfers, increased costs, and frustrated customers. The goals were to reduce the number of transfer and phone calls needed to resolve a query or to increase the FIRST/FINAL KPI and also to reduce the number of abandoned calls. The Taxpayer's Charter imposed an additional metric upon the ATO, stating that 100% of the calls would be answered in two minutes at non-busy times and 100% would be answered in five minutes in peak times.

Step Four - Measure

The ATO experienced the benefits of intelligent routing immediately. It took a few months to fine-tune their routing engines because the customer demands kept changing and the system had to be flexible. They also had a diverse set of twelve very complex products, so ramping up their people took extra time to train them, but this paid off in the end. Customer satisfaction increased: only one in every 10,000 calls is a complaint, even though they deal with 15% more calls. Figure 8.7 shows the change in occupancy and abandoned calls before and after the technology implementation. The occupancy increased from 55% to 85%. The number of abandoned calls decreased from 8% to 5%.

Step Five - Predict

As the existing telephone operations were relatively unstructured, there was little opportunity for the ATO to predict the effect of intelligent routing on the organization The lack of management reporting and the total alteration in the method of phone inquiries were handled meant that to some extent, the ATO did not really know what sort of results to expect. However, they felt that there would be substantial change and improvement going from a manual system to an automated system.

Step Six - Cost and ROI

The movement from a loose group of informal contact centers to an operation run far more tightly reduced ATO's costs very significantly (figure 8.8). The breakeven point for the ATO CRM initiative was at 2.5 months after installation. The original cost-benefit analysis took the form of a business case proposing two 125-seat call centers, which indicated a productivity savings equivalent to 25 to 50 agents per year. This was expanded once it was realized that the present adhoc way of dealing with phone inquires was actually more expensive than had been thought.

As a government organization, the ATO believed it was better to be able to manage a definite fixed cost per year and choose a five-year leasing option where the managed service provider would supply the IT equipment and software, with the ATO providing the buildings, people, and LAN operations. The ATO has also improved their customer operations, with the improvement in agent occupancy rates and reduction in abandoned calls demonstrating the higher standard of service that customers now experience. Promised service levels have also been achieved.

Step Seven - Continuous Improvement

In the years since implementation, they have saved millions in operational costs. Over ten million inbound calls have been routed using the new system. Correct routing of calls is done through the automated attendant IVR, which guides the caller to the right department. Service is provided locally through the capture of the caller's dialing code. The ATO has experienced measurable gains of over $800,000 each month. This is a positive return on investment of $12 for every $1 spent since the implementation in July 1999. This payback increased as the ATO fine-tuned their routing strategies, and in the two years since implementation, has saved almost $18 million in operational costs.

From the improvements and feedback from customers and agents in the future, the ATO is ambitious in its plans to develop its contact center service further. They are interested in implementing screen popping, and to expand their routing capabilities to balance workloads between sites.

The ATO presently makes around 50,000 outbound telephone calls per month, and will develop this further, as outbound agents can provide help and advice to six times as many customers per day when compared with traditional field workers. The trial of the outbound technology will allow greater productivity and compliance with tax regulations, while being perceived by the community as less antagonistic than a face-to-face meeting or impersonal letter.

An Internet suite is also being tested. The ATO is looking to offer integrated channels to customers. The organization wants to use their Web site as more of an interactive educational resource, where customers can serve themselves, but can be supported by the contact center when they need help. John P. Ryan, the Assistance Commissioner at ATO explains: "If our community contacts us on any one of these channels, we want to provide the same high level of experience. We see multi-channel integration as a critical part of developing our CRM strategy in terms of managing the interactions between the community and ourselves."

ROI? It's possible, but it requires that we have a strategy. We need to know specifically what business objectives we want to accomplish as well as the KPI—internal and external—to measure. Then we need to make sure someone measures the results!

In our last chapter, let's see the best way to measure our CRM center.

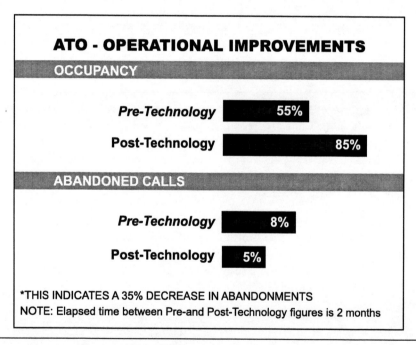

Figure 8.7. ATO operational improvements

Australian Tax Office - Cumulative Benefit

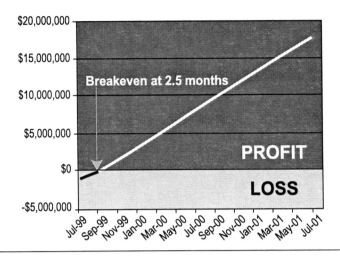

Figure 8.8. Breakeven point for ATO CRM initiative

Customer Obsession Graffiti #16

"Only through the CTI system in our call center can we provide such a unique solution for those facing fines—both court-imposed and civil—by easing the pain of face-to-face contact and making arrangements for periodic ongoing payments."
—*Helen Duckworth, Call Center Manager Collections Business Unit, New Zealand Government Agency*

Customer Obsession Graffiti #17

This account in Hull Quebec Canada had a significant RIO issue. They were contracted to provide first line support for Microsoft desktop products. Due to the number of products and no ability to do skill-based routing. Their training period was longer than their retention rate. (i.e., agents were resigning before finishing the training). We implemented skill-based routing that let us completely reverse this. Compensation was tied to training as an incentive to learn more. Staff enjoyed the environment and retention was no longer an issue.

—*Digital Equipment, Canada*

CHAPTER 9: BENCHMARKING CRM
PERFORMANCE FOR BEST PRACTICES

Certifying Your CRM Center via Benchmarking

In this chapter we look at the advantages to measuring your CRM system with respect to your peers via benchmarking. Benchmarking allows you to know where you are with respect to being CRM-centric so that you can make the changes that matter most to your customer segments (Belfiore, 2002).

Since customer service is a strategic weapon for getting, keeping, and growing profitable customers, the importance of performance benchmarking is mission critical. Peer benchmarking is a structured, analytical method of comparing the performance of two or more customer service centers in order to determine best practice goals and to ensure competitive customer relationship management functionality leading to market dominance. It is the best way to determine if the money you are spending on CRM is returning your investment and providing the customer service functions you want it to. To get out of the cost-containment rut, a customer service process needs to be assessed and the gaps in its current performance addressed so that the CRM function can then become a profit center.

Even today, there are CRM centers that do not benchmark on a regular, statistically sound basis. This is difficult to understand, given the advantages of benchmarking, which include the following (*see also figure 9.1 on the next page*):

- managerial visibility into your operations—on a quantitative basis
- comparability to competitors: how are you really performing
- pinpointing performance gaps with a high degree of precision
- targeted "calls to action": identifying and quantifying improvement initiatives
- work life improvement through identifying human resources initiatives
- career enhancement through contact center accreditation programs
- shareholder value improvement through measurable, earnings-per-share-oriented investments.

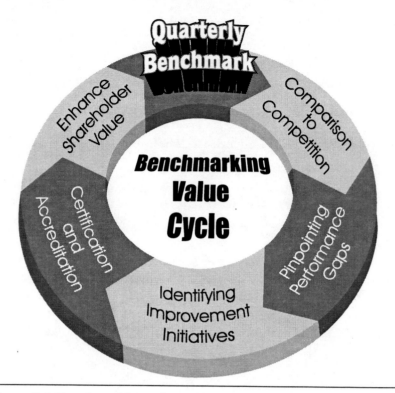

Figure 9.1. Benchmarking value cycle

It is becoming increasingly recognized that benchmarking is an essential function for a properly managed CRM center. The insights, efficiencies and aids to decision-making that are offered through benchmarking are so compelling that managers cannot do without it and still consider themselves in line with professional standards. Consider the following:

- Among **publicly quoted companies**, there is growing awareness that CRM centers are a great, untapped source of revenue enhancement, cost containment, and thus improved shareholder value. Even equity analysts are showing new interest in evaluating the competitive position of the CRM centers of the companies they analyze.

- **Privately held companies** are searching for ways to optimize all of their business areas and are finding benchmarking to be a powerful tool in optimizing customer relationships and customer lifetime value.

212

- **Government CRM centers** are reacting to mandates that they benchmark their activities against the private sector and find ways to improve service to citizens.

This represents a major change from just a few years ago. CRM centers have traditionally been under-funded, under-appreciated and misunderstood by top-level executives and by the world in general.

Selecting and Defining Performance Metrics

First we must determine which CRM center metrics to manage in the discovery process of comparing you to your peer group of CRM centers. The Purdue University Benchmark Research Web site at www.benchmarkPortal.com provides a simple and cost-effective way to create a peer benchmark report.

The metrics most important in the peer group benchmarking investigation are described in two categories below, i.e., those metrics that impact (1) efficiency, and (2) effectiveness. A very general benchmark goal is suggested for each metric; however, in the actual performance comparisons, this should be done directly with your self-defined peer group.

Effectiveness Metrics

Effectiveness metrics are those that address the caller's issues, thereby achieving the strategic goals of the CRM center: getting, growing, and keeping loyal profitable customers.

1. *Caller Satisfaction*. Most customer service centers have some method of asking callers how satisfied they were with the calling experience. Suggested measures are what percentage of callers are willing to give you a perfect score, i.e., a 5 out of 5, a 7 out of 7, or a 10 out of 10 points. This is not easy to achieve; a reasonable benchmark goal is 50%.

2. *First Customer Service Resolution*. Callers want their issue resolved with only one customer service call to your company (also called "first-time-final" or "once-and-done" calls). This means no transfers and no callbacks. A good benchmark target for this metric is 85%.

3. *Percentage of Calls Blocked*. This is a measure of caller accessibility. By dividing the volume of calls handled by the calls offered, the percentage of calls blocked is determined. A target goal for this metric should be under 4%.

213

4. *Average Speed of Answer (ASA)*. Average speed of answer (ASA) is also a measurement of customer accessibility when managed to a X- or X-hour increment. ASA is determined by dividing the total-queue-time by the total calls handled for the measurement period. A good benchmark is 18 seconds, managed to the half-hour period.

5. *Service Level (SL)*. As with ASA, service level is also a measurement of caller accessibility. SL is computed by determining the percentage of calls that are answered within X number of seconds in a distinct period of time. Also, as with ASA, it is critical to manage SL to a one-half- or one-quarter-hour period, which ties the measurement to the customer experience. A common benchmark target is 80% answered in 20 seconds managed to the half-hour period.

6. *Percentage of Calls Leading to an Up-Sell or a Cross-Sell*. As customer service centers move from cost centers to profit centers, a measure of effectiveness is the ability to detect opportunities for making sales. A benchmark for this metric, in excess of 20% of calls, should result in an opportunity to at least do an "up-sell" to the caller.

Specific Efficiency Metrics

Efficiency metrics focus on achieving the CRM center's effectiveness goals as inexpensively as possible. Some of the important efficiency metrics are as follows:

1. *Calls Handled per Shift*. This metric will vary widely depending on the industry studied. If we study all respondents in our benchmark database, the average is 43 calls per shift.

2. *Percentage of Callers That Abandon*. If a caller accesses the customer service center ACD, is then placed into a queue and not handled by an agent within an acceptable time, the caller will hang up, or abandon from queue. The percentage of abandons is a good measure of how efficiently the center is managed. The benchmark is less than 4% for abandoned calls.

3. *Average Talk Time (ATT)*. Average talk time represents the amount of time an agent is engaged with a caller. The metric usually includes conversation time and hold time (when the agent puts the caller on hold to ask a question, access reference material, etc.). It does not include queue time. ATT varies considerably with the industry segment and purpose of

the call. An all-industry benchmark would be less than 5 minutes.

4. *After Call Work Time (ACW)*. After call work time is the time an agent spends completing a transaction precipitated by a phone call after the call is released. The benchmark goal should be less than 3 minutes.

5. *Percentage Occupancy*. The formula for occupancy is talk time plus after call work time divided by talk time plus after call work time plus time waiting for calls. The target for this metric should be at 90%.

6. *Cost per Call*. Cost per call is a figure that most customer service centers are able to compute. It is determined by dividing the operating budget by the number of calls handled by the center. Although it varies widely, the fully loaded average for all industries is about $7 per call.

7. *Percentage Calls Handled by Self Service*. The percentage of all calls that are handled by the IVR unit is an indication of efficiency. The target benchmark for this metric should be 20% or more.

8. *Percentage Schedule Adherence*. Schedule adherence ties directly to the management of the forecasting and scheduling process. Once a schedule is created that determines when each agent should be at his or her position and available to take calls, this metric monitors how well the agents adhere to that schedule. Most companies set a 95% target, meaning that each agent is logged onto or off of the system, within the leeway of 1 to 3 minutes, 95% of the time.

9. *Annual Turnover Percentage*. Employee turnover is normal, and should be expected in any company. However, an excessive rate of turnover can hurt a company financially. The benchmark is less than 10% turnover per year (leaving the company). This does not include movement to other areas of the company or promotions.

The Case Study Organizational Profile

This case study describes the benchmarking experience of a CRM center in a banking and financial services organization in North America. This company, with $3 billion in assets, operated 22 customer service centers and employed 325 telephone service representatives who annually handled 4,524,000 calls. The primary functions of these representatives were customer service and

215

handling complaints. Ninety percent of the calls they handled were inbound. The other 10 percent were follow-up outbound calls.

This bank participated in the Purdue benchmark research and has given its permission to use the data without revealing the identity of the bank. The Purdue benchmarking team selected a peer group, that is, a group of customer service centers with a similar profile to this bank's call center. The profile delimiters used were industry segment (that is, banking and financial services), number of inbound calls handled (in this case, 2 million to 5 million calls), number of telephone service representatives (200 to 400), type of calls handled, and many more.

The next sections of this case study will:

- give examples of the reports the bank's benchmark team used to change performance
- explain the initiatives selected by the benchmarking team
- report on the final actual improvements in performance that resulted six months later.

Selecting Improvement Initiatives

Once you have entered the benchmark data via this online process, you get a profile of the call center. In the profile are several reports that can help a company determine the improvement initiatives to begin with. Those are the:

1. Peer Group Performance Matrix
2. Inbound Performance Comparison Report
3. Performance Ranking Report
4. Peer Group Performance Matrix

1. Peer Group Performance Matrix

The first report shows the peer group performance matrix shown in figure 9.2.

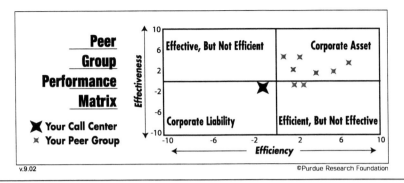

Figure 9.2. Peer Group Performance Matrix

This report uses an efficiency index. An efficiency index is a combination of ten performance metrics that are related to productivity. Examples would be average talk time, average after call work time, and calls per telephone service representative per shift.

To create this matrix, the efficiency index is plotted on the x-axis, and the effectiveness index is plotted on the y-axis. Customer service centers that are very inefficient at doing a very ineffective job for their companies are considered a corporate liability, whereas customer service centers that are very efficient and doing a very effective job for their companies are considered a corporate asset.

The performance matrix shows that the case study bank's customer service center is performing at the level of a corporate liability, while six of its peer group customer service centers achieved the status of a corporate asset. Two of the peer group customer service centers are in the efficient but not effective quadrant. It is immediately obvious to the benchmarking team that they must drill down to determine what factors are causing this less-than-acceptable performance.

Although the peer group performance matrix is not an actionable report, it is a high-level and accurate litmus test of the call center's ability to provide the customer-relationship-management best-practice standards of peer group customer service centers with the same business challenges. So, the next step is to find one or more of the possible root causes of the low performance.

2. The Inbound Performance Comparison Report

The first drill-down report is called the "Inbound Performance Comparison Report." Figure 9.3 shows a partial listing from this report. The peer group best is the top ten percent of a peer group.

Inbound Performance Comparisons

Metric Description	Your Center Response	Peer Group Median	Peer Group Average	Peer Group Best Median	Peer Group Best Average	All Participants Median	All Participants Average
Average Speed of Answer (seconds)	15.0	20.0	32.2	12.5	17.1	25.0	33.3
Average Talk Time (minutes)	9.1	3.0	7.2	3.0	3.4	4.0	10.2
Average After Call Work Time (minutes)	3.0	1.0	5.3	1.0	1.1	2.0	6.8
Average Calls Abandoned (%)	6.0	3.0	5.0	2.0	2.8	4.7	5.5
Average Time in Queue (seconds)	20.0	35.0	44.3	16.0	18.4	34.0	43.2
Average First/Final Calls (%)	65.0	79.0	77.3	85.0	86.1	79.0	68.1
Average TSR Occupancy (%)	60.0	80.0	79.4	87.0	89.1	79.0	74.9
Average Adherence to Schedule (%)	82.0	89.0	87.8	92.0	95.3	84.1	86.0
Average Calls/Shift/TSR (calls)	58.0	70.0	83.2	85.0	86.5	70.0	69.2
Average Attendance (%)	75.0	90.0	88.7	95.0	87.7	88.3	86.9

v.9.02 ©Purdue Research Foundation

Figure 9.3. Excerpt from the Inbound Performance Comparison Report

This report shows the following:

- customer service center performance metrics descriptions in the first column

- a column with the actual customer service center performance metrics (noted as "Your Center")

- the peer group medians and averages

- the best in peer group medians and averages

- the average for all participants.

For brevity purposes, this excerpt shows only ten customer service center performance metrics that highlight management opportunities. It immediately became clear to the benchmarking team that the customer service center is under performing on the following metrics:

- average speed of answer
- average calls abandoned
- average time-in-queue
- average first/final calls
- average telephone service representative occupancy
- average adherence to schedule
- average calls per shift per telephone representative.

218

At this stage of the drill-down research by the benchmarking team, it was already becoming clear which metric might be having the biggest impact on performance and customer service. The most important caller satisfaction driver is the ability of a customer service center to answer callers' questions on the first call with no transfers and no callbacks. In figure 9.3, this metric is called the "average first/final calls" (also sometimes called "average once-and-done calls"). The bank's score is 65% compared with the score of 77.3% for the peer groups of banks. The difference of 12.3% may appear small, but when the cost of this lack of performance is calculated for this bank, it totals over $2 million each year. That expense makes it worth launching an improvement initiative.

3. The Performance Ranking Report

The second drill-down report is called the Peer Group Ranking Report. Figure 9.4 gives a partial listing of this report.

Metrics ▸	Blocked Calls	Adherence	ASA	ATT	Abandoned	Queue Time	Occupancy
Your Percentile ▸	95.7%	26%	87%	22%	52.1%	74.0%	18%
1	.04%	95%	5	2.2	0%	10	91
2	1.85%	94%	7	3.6	2%	11	88
3	2.81%	92%	10	3.7	2%	13	86
4	3.05%	91%	15	4.2	2%	15	85
5	3.17%	90%	22	4.9	3%	16	82
Rank 6	4.84%	90%	25	5.1	4%	20	77
7	5.80%	89%	31	5.3	5%	32	73
8	5.82%	88%	31	6.6	6%	36	71
9	6.45%	86%	50	7.3	7%	39	68
10	7.78%	82%	60	8.5	7%	42	63
11	8.44%	77%	68	9.1	9%	45	60

©Purdue Research Foundation

Figure 9.4. Excerpt from the Peer Group Ranking Report

This report gives the benchmarking team an even more granular look at how the bank compares, metric for metric, with its peer group of banks. For instance, when it comes to blocked calls, the case study bank is actually doing rather well, performing in the 95.7 percentile and ranking second. However, in the important performance metric of telephone representative occupancy, the bank is ranked only 11th, and only in the 18th percentile.

The team wanted to select the one metric that may be causing the most damage to performance—that is, finding the lowest hanging fruit—so management can direct a focused budget for an improvement initiative. Again, we want to point out that CRM is about change—changing the way service is being provided.

219

This is why we spent so much time previously discussing the nature of change. Measurement can tell you what to change, but not how to go about making the changes so that they are accepted and not sabotaged. Not shown in figure 9.4 is that the bank ranks at the bottom, having had the absolute worst performance, on the metric of "average first/final calls." That initiative became the focus of the bank's benchmarking team.

4. Performance Gaps to Solution Initiative Optimizer

The final report is called the Gap versus Solution Optimizer report. A partial listing of this report appears in figure 9.5.

Gap vs Solution Optimizer

GAP: "Once & Done Calls"	SOLUTION	Cost Per Seat ($)	Implement Time (days)	Risk Factor (0-100)	Gap Impact (%)	ROI (%)	Optimal Decision
	Applicant Testing	100	30	40	20	374	6.49
	Skill Based Routing	400	50	50	75	315	4.51
	Applicant Screening	250	40	30	30	184	2.18
	CT Integration	900	120	75	90	137	1.91
	Value Based Routing	400	60	60	55	128	1.49
	Monitoring/Coaching	300	60	40	65	118	1.33
	Product Training	600	90	65	35	91	1.01
	Expert Systems	1500	180	95	55	89	.94
	Contract Tracking	3000	120	85	50	64	.85
	Performance Comp	300	30	10	15	64	.65
	CB Training	600	90	35	35	53	.61

v.9.02   ©Purdue Research Foundation

Figure 9.5. Excerpt from the Gap versus Solution Optimizer report

This report gives the benchmark team a listing of all gaps in excess of 20% (that is, the major ones). For each gap it provides a list of potentially applicable solutions to reduce that gap. The figure lists only one such gap—"percent of once-and-done calls"—although there were a total of eight major gaps in performance at the bank's customer service center that required their own list of optimized solutions.

From the previous reports, the benchmarking team decided that the biggest negative gap in performance seems to be the average first/final calls, or "once-and-done calls." The Gap versus Solution Optimizer report then became a management aid to select that one solution that may produce the best results with the minimum corporate resources.

This reports lists 11 solutions that could be implemented in the order of most desirable on the basis of the optimal decision index. This index is calculated by statistically averaging the most important issues that managers should consider when selecting any improvement initiative:

- **Cost per seat:** Many solutions are priced on the basis of cost per seat. Knowing this factor allows the manager to quickly determine if there is enough money in the budget to even consider the initiative.
- **Implementation time:** This is an estimate of the average implementation time to complete the installation of the solution. Most managers prefer to select initiatives that can be implemented within approximately six months.
- **Risk factor:** Most managers are risk averse. The risk factor has been developed over time by discussion solutions with those who have already implemented a solution. Sometimes high-risk solutions are worth undertaking, but only in light of the other decision factors.
- **Gap impact factor:** This factor gives an indication of the percent of the gap that will be reduced by the successful implementation of a particular solution.
- **Return-on-investment (ROI):** This is the standard ROI equation that decision-makers use most often in selecting one solution over another.

From the Gap versus Solution Optimizer report it becomes clear that applicant testing and skill-based routing are high on the list of potential improvement initiatives. In this particular example, the bank's benchmarking team received management's approval to pursue both initiatives. Specifications were prepared, a request-for-proposal (RFP) was issued, vendors were selected, and the initiatives were launched and successfully completed.

Monitoring Improvement Processes

It is important to not only make the changes, but also to monitor the changes over time to ensure they produce the desired results. In this case, six months after the successful installation and implementation of the two improvement initiatives, the following results were tabulated:

- The percentage of first/final calls improved by 11.6%.
- The average time in queue was reduced by 2.8%.
- The average TSR occupancy improved by just over 6%.
- Calls per TSRs per shift increased by 9.4%.
- Caller satisfaction rose by almost 7%.

The bank spent approximately $600,000 for the two improvement initiatives, including the selection process, the cost of the software and hardware products, the training costs of the TSRs, and the installation services costs from a third-party integrator. When the improved metrics were converted to new revenue, reduced operating cost, and customer satisfaction, the estimated ROI was in excess of 100% in 16 months of operation.

Benchmarking cannot guarantee the success of any improvement initiative. However, this case study does prove that by scientifically selecting initiatives based on hard facts, not just personal intuition or gut feel, management can effectively target improvements that have the maximum impact on the company's profits.

Setting Balanced Priorities for Both CRM Quality and Corporate Profits

Benchmarking must be part of a value circle that includes the following elements:

1. *Self-awareness*. Managers should use benchmarking of all contact center processes to gain awareness and a clearer vision of how well their center operates. We find that the simple act of gathering and entering data can provide numerous points of revelation for management and analytical staff. Do not shy away from these insights. Equally, do not be surprised if some of these insights are a bit cloudy the first time you benchmark. You *will* get better at it, and you *will* garner useful, actionable information to reduce costs and increase effectiveness, and thereby, quality.

2. *Comparability to Competitors*. The perennial question: "How good is good enough?" is key for center managers. You need to match or just beat the competition and customer expectations. You do *not* need to be perfect. Perfection is not only impossible; it is extremely costly to attempt. Yet you will never know what the proper "bar level" is if you do not benchmark against your appropriate peer group. Peer groups are essential, since the relevant competitive metrics for your center will depend heavily on factors like industry, function, and geography.

3. *Pinpointing Opportunities*. All contact centers experience operational performance gaps. Everyone will have his or her own analysis of what those gaps are. Since our sector is full of highly verbal people who continually deal with human

222

emotions and needs, there will be a lot of advice coming your way, often based more on gut feelings than on facts. Benchmarking provides the hard numbers that either statistically validate those gut feelings or point the way to other, more important issues. Competitive gaps show up very clearly in the metrics!

4. *Identifying Improvement Initiatives*. Our benchmarking reports include the "Solutions Index," which lays out specific solutions for negative competitive gaps. This is the place to start for spending your precious technology and training budgets. Remember, experts state that upwards of 60% of all customer relationship management investments are failures or do not provide the expected improvements! Metric-based and performance-targeted initiatives will help you move from poor performance to best practices.

5. *Post-Implementation Benchmarking*. After you have implemented an improvement initiative, you should benchmark again to determine the impact of the initiative. Now you have completed the first full "value circle"!

6. *Accreditation and Certification*. A conscientiously applied improvement program should also include upgrading of human resources through professional certification programs (whether in-person or distance learning), certification of processes and, ultimately, accreditation of the contact center as a whole. A commitment to certification and accreditation is the best way to ensure that continuous improvement benchmarking becomes part of the DNA of your contact center management. This, in turn, will result in improved operations, careers, and shareholder value; in a word: success! We recommend that you make that commitment today.

The key uses of performance benchmarking are:

1. Better understanding contact center processes by establishing key performance indicators to guide management decisions.

2. Reducing bureaucratic barriers to change by spotlighting performance gaps, and stating the gaps in financial terms, i.e., dollars lost.

3. Pinpointing the one initiative that commits a minimum of resources to achieve the maximum cost savings and improved quality.

223

The end of our journey has come upon us. However, your journey for CRM has just begun as you finish reading this book. We've started you out by looking at the strategic business objectives and given you our magic squares to follow through on your planning, build/deploy, and maintenance. We've discovered the resistance of people/employees to changes in how they do their job. We've also looked at the impact of business process mapping on customer accessibility. The last half of the book was on the operational and analytical technology and its various uses to increase customer accessibility, satisfaction and lifetime value. In our last chapters we've shown how ROI can be obtained and in how to know by benchmarking and measuring how you are truly doing on an ongoing basis. We wish you the best of luck and may you have many wonderful experiences on the journey to CRM success!

Customer Obsession Graffiti #18

"Use of the new system has helped bring the ratio (sales conversion rate) up while the cost of doing business has gone down. The result is a much higher rate of sales and a lower cost of acquisition."
—*Tony Cooke, Business Development Manager, SalesForce, Inc.*

Customer Obsession Graffiti #19

"As customers become more sophisticated and better informed about their choices, an organization can no longer compete simply on price or product," says Leonia Bank's Vice President, Arto Smedberg. The bank has established telephone and Web-based banking services for customers who prefer to use these channels.

The challenge Leonia faced was how to maximize these channels—both of which are far more cost-effective ways to conduct business than the traditional branch network—without damaging its own market share and reputation.

Leonia needed to reduce the number of branches while increasing the ease with which customers can do business over the phone or Internet. Key to the success of this strategy was ensuring that those customers affected by branch closures would not see or perceive a decline in service levels—a problem that has befallen many banks. In light of this, Leonia made a number of strategic decisions:

- Facilitate telephone and Internet banking for services such as balance inquiries, bill payments, investments and the movement of funds.

- Encourage customers to adopt different channels for conducting banking services (i.e., offer Internet training courses to its customers to encourage doing business over the Internet).

—*Leonia Bank's Vice President, Arto Smedberg*

1. APT Data Group. 1996. "Briefing Paper: What is Meta Data?" (March).

2. Alder, Paul S. 1997. *Perspectives on work.* Center For Human Resources at the Wharton School and Institute for Work and Employment Research 1:61.

3. Amen, Daniel G. 1998. *Change Your Brain, Change Your Life.* New York: Random.

4. Anderson, Paul and Art Rosenberg. 2000. *The Executive's Guide To CRM.* Houston, Texas: Doyle Publishing Company, Inc.

5. Anton, Jon. 1997. *Call Center Management By The Numbers.* West Lafayette, Indiana: Ichor Business Books, Purdue University Press.

6. Anton, Jon. 1999. *Call Center Performance Enhancement: Using Simulation and Modeling.* West Lafayette, Indiana: Ichor Business Books, Purdue University Press.

7. Anton, Jon. 1997. *Listening to the Voice of the Customer.* New York: The Customer Service Group.

8. Anton, Jon. 1994. Internal research report. (May) West Lafayette, IN: Purdue University Center for Custom-Driven Quality.

9. Anton, Jon., R. Bennett, and R. Widdows. 1994. *Call-Center Design and Implementation.* Houston, TX: Dame Publications.

10. Anton, Jon., and David Gustin. 2000. *Call Center Benchmarking: How Good Is Good Enough?".* West Lafayette, Indiana: Ichor Business Books, Purdue University Press.

11. Anton, Jon., and J.C. de Ruyter. 1991. Van Klachten naar Managementinformatie. *Harvard Holland Review* 27 (Fall).

12. Anton, Jon. and Natalie L. Petouhoff. 2001. *CRM: The Bottom-line To Optimizing Your ROI.* Upper Saddle River: Prentice Hall.

13. Anton, Jon, Natalie L. Petouhoff and Lisa M. Schwartz. 2002. *Integrating People, Processes and CRM Technology.* Santa Maria, CA, Anton Press.

14. Anton, Jon, and Julie Kuliopulos. "The Valley of Tears," *Teleprofessional,* 1998.

15. Baldwin, Howard. 2002. "Prescription for Healthier CRM." *Enterprise.* (March 18, 2002).

16. Barker, Joel. 1993. *Paradigms: The Business of Discovering the Future.* New York: Harper and Row.

17. Barlett, Christopher A. 1996. Changing the role of top management beyond systems to people. *Harvard Business Review.* (January).

18. Belfiore, Bruce. 2002. *Benchmarking for Profits!* Santa Maria, CA, Anton Press.

19. Berry, John. 2001. IT Dividends: IT ROI metrics fall into four groups. *Internet Week* 45 (July 16, 2001).

20. Berry, L. L. 1988. Delivering excellent service in retailing. Arthur Andersen Retailing Issues Letter (April).

21. Berry, L. L., and A. Parasuraman. 1991. *Marketing Services.* New York: The Free Press.

22. Betts, M. 1993. Real IS payoff lies in business benefits. *Computerworld* 56 (March).

23. Bhote, Keki R. 1996. *Beyond Customer Satisfaction To Customer Loyalty.* New York: American Management Association.

24. Block, Peter. 1991. *The Empowered Manager.* New York: Jossey-Bass.

25. Block, Peter. 1996. *Stewardship: Choosing Service Over Self Interest.* New York: Berrett-Koehler.

26. Brown, Dave. 2001. Re-engineering Timberline customer service from mediocre to award winning. *Customer Support Management* 36 (January).

27. Buckingham, Marcus, and Curt Coffman. 1999. *First Break All The Rules.* New York: Simon & Schuster.

28. Cantin, M. 1986. The Heart As An Endocrine Gland. *Clinical and Investigative Medicine.* No. 4, 319.

29. Capra, Fritjof. 1996. *The Web of Life.* New Work: Anchor Books.

30. Carr, Eric. 2001. "CRM in No Time Flat?" *Smart Partner.* (September 5, 2001).

31. Caulfield, Brian. 2001. Pricey new CRM technology tracks customers, but will it add to the bottom-line? *Business 2.0* 149 (August/September).

32. Chase, Richard. 2001. Using Behavioral Science to Boost CRM: feelings are critical to CRM. *ComputerWorld* 50 (June 4, 2001).

33. Childre, Doc and Bruce Cryer. 1999. *From Chaos To Coherence: Advancing Emotional and Organizational Intelligence Through Inner Quality Management.* Boston: Butterworth-Heinemann.

34. Clark, T. 1993. Marketing key to HP's battle plan. *Business Marketing* 15 (July).

35. Clemmer, J. 1993. Making change work: Integrating focus, effort, and direction. *Canadian Business Review* 30 (Winter).

36. Cooper, Robert. 1997. *Executive EQ: Emotional Intelligence In Leadership and Organizations.* New York: Grosset/Putnam.

37. Covey, Stephen. 1990. *Seven Habits of Highly Effective People.* New York: Simon & Schuster.

38. Cronin, J. J., and S. A. Taylor. 1992. Measuring service quality. *Journal of Marketing* 56 (July).

39. Davidow, W. H. and B. Uttal. 1989. *Total Customer Service.* New York: Harper and Row.

40. Davis, T. R. V. 1992. Satisfying internal customers: The link to external customer satisfaction. *Planning Review* 35 (January/February).

41. DCI Conference, 2001. Customer Relationship Management. Los Angeles. (December 11-14, 2001).

42. de Bono, Edward. 1999. *Six Thinking Hat Processes.* New York: Little Brown and Company.

43. Devlin, Barry. 1999. "From Data Model to Data Warehouse in Bite-Sized Chunks!" *Info DB*, Vol. 9, No. 5.

44. Dicksteen, Lisa Napell. 2001. Virtual Roundtable: CRM across multiple channels. *Customer Support Management* 45 (January).

45. Drucker, P. F. 1979 *Adventures of a Bystander.* New York: Harper & Row.

46. Dunn, Jim. 2001. Assessing your spend in the new frontier: eCRM. *iSource Business: Online Supply Chain Solutions* 69 (August).

47. Dutka, A. 1993. *AMA Handbook for Customer Satisfaction.* Lincolnwood, IL:NTC Publishing Group.

48. Earl, Micheal and David Feeny. 2000. "How To Be a CEO for the Information Age." *Sloan Management Review.* Winter.

49. Ehrbar, Al, 1998. *Economic Value Added: The Real Key To Creating Wealth.* New York: Wiley and Sons, Inc.

50. Eisler, Riane. 1995. *The Chalice and the Blade.* New York: Harper and Row.

51. Ehrenman, Gayle. 2001. CRM facts: companies spending more on CRM. *Internet Week* 17 (July 16, 2001).

52. Ernst & Young Survey. 1990. Biggest challenge for next five years. *Electronic Business Magazine* 33 (March).

53. Fabris, Peter. 1998. "Data Mining," *CIO Magazine* (May 15, 1998).

54. Feinberg, R., and R. Widdows. (n.d). The critical incident technique. *Mobious* 8.2, 8.

55. The Financial Accounting Standards Board. 1999. Measuring the invisibles. *Business Spirit Journal* (March/April): 1. Also see <*www.bizspirit.com*>.

56. Fournies, Ferdinand. 1999. *Why Employees Don't Do What They're Supposed to Do and What to Do About It.* New York: McGraw-Hill.

57. Freedman, D. H. 1993. A model worth copying. *CIO Magazine* 42 (August).

58. Gale, B.T. 1992. Relative perceived quality. *Planning Review* 7 (July/August).

59. "Gallup Organization: New Research Links Emotional Intelligence With Profitability." 1998. *The Inner Edge Journal* (December): 5. Also see <*www.gallup.com*>.

60. Gentry, Jeff. 2001. "The Business Intelligence Justification Forest." Enterprise Systems (December).

61. Glanz, Barbara. 1996. *Care Packages for the Workplace: Dozens of Little things You Can Do To Regenerate Spirit at Work.* New York: McGraw-Hall.

62. Goleman, Daniel. 1995, 1998. *Emotional Intelligence and Working With Emotional Intelligence.* New York: Bantam Books.

63. Hamilton-Smith, K., and T. Morris. 1993. Market-driven quality. *CMA Magazine* 24 (May).

64. Harris, A.S. 1991. The customer's always right. *Black Enterprises* 234 (June).

65. Hawkin, Paul. 1993. *The Ecology of Commerce: A Declaration of Sustainability.* New York: HarperBusiness.

66. HeartMath. 2001. Conversations with Bruce Cryer. P.O. Box 1463 14700 W. Park Ave, Boulder Creek, CA 95006. 408-338-8700 < www.heartmath.com>

67. Heskett, J., W. E. Sasser, and L. Schlesinger. 1997 *The Service Profit Chain.* New York: The Free Press.

68. Hubbard, Barbara Marx. 1998. *Conscious Evolution: Awakening the Power of Our Social Potential.* Novato, CA: New World Library.

69. Hughes, D.H. 1992. We can't get there from here. *CMA Magazine* 12 (November).

70. Huson, Stephen. 1998. "Diamond in the Rough: Bringing to Light Customer Information through Data Mining," *Call Center Solutions,* Vol. 17, No. 1, p. 104. (July).

71. The INC/Gallup Survey. *INC Magazine* 1996, 1997, 1998, 1999, 2000 and 2001.

72. Inmon, Bill. 1998. "Getting Around Dormant Data," *Teradata Review,* Summer.

73. James, Geoffrey. 2002. "Profit Motive: How to Get The Most Benefit From Your CRM Investment," Selling Power. (March).

74. Javid, Shawn. 1999. "Data Mining in the Next Millennium," *DM Direct,* (October).

75. Jenkins, Drury. 1999. "Customer Relationship Management and the Data Warehouse," *Call Center Solutions,* p. 88. (August).

76. Jupiter Media Metrix. 2001. Harte Hanks. Found in CRM facts: companies spending more on CRM. *Internet Week* 17 (July 16, 2001).

77. Kanigel, Robert. 1997. *The One Best Way: Frederick Winslow Taylor and the Enigma of Efficiency.* New York: Viking Penguin.

78. Kimball, Ralph. 1998. "Meta Meta Data Data," *DBMS*, (March).

79. Knauer, V. 1992. *Increasing Customer Satisfaction*. Pueblo, CO: United States Office of Consumer Affairs.

80. Kotter, John. 1995. Leading change: Why transformations efforts fail. *Harvard Business Review* (January).

81. Kurtyka, Jerry. 1999. "Customer Knowledge Management," *Knowledge Management*, p. 85. (December).

82. Lawton, L. 1991. Creating a customer-centered culture in service industries. *Quality Process* 71 (September).

83. Learning, Motivation, and Results. LMR Associates.com 2001. Private conversations with Lana Ruffins. 8306 Wilshire Blvd, Suite 78, Beverly Hills, CA 90211. 1-323-RESULTS. <*www.lmrassociates.com*>.

84. Lian, T. 1994. Helping hands. *Bank Marketing* 25 (February).

85. Lichtenberg, Ronna. 1998. *Work Would Be Great If It Weren't For The People*. New York: Hyperion.

86. Lewis, David. 2001. Top executives rein in CIOs on technology projects: demand ROI. *Internet Week* 1 (July 16, 2001).

87. Lloyd-Williams, Michael. 1997. "Discovering the Hidden Secrets in Your Data: The Data Mining Approach to Information," Department of Information Studies, University of Sheffield. (May).

88. Mackay, H. 1993. *Swim With The Sharks Without Being Eaten Alive*. New York: William Morrow & Company.

89. MacIver, Kenny. 1999. "Universal Intelligence," *Global Technology Business*, Vol. 2, No. 9.

90. Manganaris, Stefanos. 2000. "Data Mining for Unusual Events," DB2 Magazine. Spring.

91. Mather, H. F. 1993. Do more than just satisfy your customers—profitably delight them. *Industrial Marketing* 11 (March/April).

92. Marston, William. 1928. *The Emotions of Normal People*. Boston: Harvard Press.

93. McCraty, Rollin. 1996. Music Enhances the Effect of Positive emotional States on Salivary IgA and Heart Rate Variability. *Stress Medicine*. 167 (December).

94. McCraty, Rollin. 1998. The Effect of Emotions on Heart Rate Variability. *American Journal of Cardiology*. No. 14, 1088 (November 15).

95. McGarvey, R. 1995. The big thrill. *Entrepreneur* 86 (July).

96. Mello, Adrian. 2002. "Six Mistakes That Will Sink Your CRM." Enterprise. (March 18, 2001).

97. Millar, Bill. 2000. The challenges of business-to-business CRM on line. *1 to 1 Direct* 27 (November).

98. Moxon, Bruce. 1996. "Defining Data Mining," *DBMS Data Warehouse Supplement*, (August).

99. Myron, David. 2002. "Size Doesn't Matter: DCI Show Serves Up A Content-Rich CRM Agenda," *Customer Relationship Management*. (February).

100. Nelson, Bob. 1994. *1001 Ways To Reward Employees*. New York: Workman Publishing.

101. Oakley, Ed and Doug Krug. 1991. *Enlightened Leadership*. New York: Simon and Schuster.

102. Ornstein, Robert. 1991. *The Evolution of Consciousness: The Origins of The Way We Think*. New York: Touchstone.

103. Osterfelt, Susan. "Business Intelligence: Mining the Whole Enchilada," *DM Review*. March 1998.

104. Panepinto, J. 1994. Going out on a wireless. *Computerworld* 99 (February).

105. Parsaye, K. "A Characterization of Data Mining Technologies and Processes," *Information Discovery Inc.*, 1998.

106. Peters, Tom. 1988. *Thriving on Chaos*. New York: Harper and Row.

107. Peter, J.P., and J.C. Olson. *Consumer Behavior and Marketing Strategy*, Irwin, 4th ed., 1996.

108. Phillips, Jack and Natalie Petouhoff. 2001. *Recruiting and Retaining Call Center Employees*. Alexander, Virginia. ASTD.

109. Phillips, Jack. 1997. *Return on Investment in Training and Performance Improvement Programs*. Houston, Texas: Gulf Publishing.

110. Plotkin, Harris. 1997. *Building a Winning Team*. New York: Griffin.

111. Plymire, J. 1991. Complaints as opportunities. *Business Horizons* 80. (March/April).

112. Pribram, Karl H. 1971. *Languages of the Brain.* New York: Brandon House.

113. PricewaterhouseCoopers. 1995. *Better Change: Best Practices for Transforming Your Organization*, PriceWaterhouse, and *The Paradox Principle: How Companies Manage Change*, PW. New York. PriceWaterhouse Publishing.

114. Prichett, Price. 1994. *New Work Habits For A Radically Changing World.* Dallas, Texas: Pritchett and Associates.

115. Reichheld, F. F. 1996. *The Loyalty Effect: The Hidden Force Behind Growth, Profits, and Lasting Value.* Boston: Harvard Business School Press.

116. Reichheld, F. F., and W. E. Sasser Jr. 1990. Zero defects: Quality comes to services. *Harvard Business Review* 106 (September/October).

117. Rein, Glen. 1995. The physiological and psychological effects of compassion and anger. *Journal of Advancement in Medicine.* No.2, 87 (August.)

118. Ritt, Thomas C. 1980. *Understanding Yourself and Others.* Tequesta, Florida: People Concepts.

119. Rosenfeld, S. A. 1977. *Conversations Between Heart and the Brain.* Rockville, Maryland: National Institute of Health.

120. Rosener, Judy. 1997. *America's Competitive Secret: Women Managers.* Oxford: Oxford University Press.

121. Rosener, Judy. 1990. Ways women lead. *Harvard Business Review* (November/December).

122. Rosener, Judy. 1991. *Workforce America! Managing Employee Diversity as a Vital Resource.* New York: Business One Irwin.

123. Rust, R. T., A. J. Zahorik, and T. L Keiningham. 1994. *Return on Quality.* Chicago: Probus Publishing Company.

124. Sager, I. 1994. The few, the true, the blue. *Business Week* 124 (May 30).

125. Senge, Peter. 1994. *The Fifth Discipline: The Art and Practice of the Learning Organization.* New York: Doubleday.

126. Seybold, Patricia B. 1998. *Customers.com.* New York: Random House.

127. Shetty, Y. K. 1993. The quest for quality excellence: Lessons from the Malcolm Baldrige Quality Award. *Advanced Management Journal* 37 (Spring).

128. Shrednick, H. R. 1995. A decade of improvements. *Information Week* 112 (January 30).

129. Shycon, H. N. 1992. Improving customer service: Measuring the payoff. *Journal of Business Strategy* 15 (January/February).

130. Sims, David. 2001. "CRM Vendors Don't Walk the Talk." *CMRGuru.com.* (October 29, 2001).

131. Soley, Alex. 1999. "Wired to be Smart," *Global Technology Business*, Vol. 2, No. 9.

132. Smith, Mark. 1999. "Why Cold Statistics Alone Don't Make Hot Marketing," *DM Direct*, April.

133. Spector, P.E. (n.d.). Summated rating scale construction: An introduction paper series on quantitative applications in the social services. Series Number 07–082. Newbury Park, CA: Sage University.

134. Spiegel, Rob. 2001. Investing for a lifetime: CRM. *iSource Business: Online Supply Chain Solutions* 55 (August).

135. Strassmann, Paul. 2001. Corporate IT budgets and spending focus. *ComputerWorld* 48 (June 4, 2001).

136. Tanaka, J. 1991. Going for the glory. *Business Week* 60 (October).

137. Tannen, Deborah. 1990. You Just Don't Understand: Women and Men In Conversation. New York: Ballantine Books.

138. Taylor, Frederick W. 1911. *The Principles of Scientific Management*. Reprint, New York: Dover, 1998.

139. Tehrani, N. 1993. Customer service & inbound telemarketing . . . The new powerful way to expand market share. *Telemarketing* 76 (March).

140. Timm, Paul. 1995. 50 Powerful Ideas You Can Use TO Keep Your Customers. 2nd edition. New Jersey: Book-mart Press.

141. Tschohl, J. 1993. For service that sells, you need service strategy. *Chain Store Age Executive* 60 (June).

142. Trombly, Maria. 2001. "Connecting With The Top Brass." Computerworld. June 4, 2001.

143. Ulrich, Dave. 1999. *Delivering Results.* Boston: Harvard Business Review Press.

144. Waxer, Cindy. 2001. Moving to the head of the class: ROI and technology. *iSource Business: Online Supply Chain Solutions* 32 (August).

145. Wisbach, Heide. 2001. How much CRM is enough in relative terms. *Marketing News.* 1 (May 7, 2001)

146. Wheatley, Margaret J. 1994. *Leadership and the New Science: Learning about Organization from An Orderly Universe.* San Francisco: Berrett-Koehler.

147. Whyte, David. 1996. *The Heart Aroused: Poetry and the Preservation of the Soul in Corporate America.* Chicago: Doubleday.

148. Whyte, William H. Jr. 1956. *The Organization Man.* New York: Doubleday.

149. Whyte, William H. Jr. 1956. The organization man. *Fortune Magazine.* (June)

150. Williamson, M. 1993. Golden handcuffs. *CIO Magazine* 48, 49.

151. Zaren, Jane E. 2001. Top eService initiatives: top technology vs. poor customer service. *Customer Support Management* S2 (January).

152. Zeithaml, V., A. Parasuraman, L. L. Berry 1990. *Delivering Quality Service.* New York: The Free Press.

153. Zetlin, Minda. 2001. 100 best places to work in IT: model employers. *ComputerWorld* 40 (June 4, 2001).

154. Zukav, Gary. 1989. *The Seat of The Soul.* New York: Fireside Simon and Schuster.

Co-Author

Dr. Jon Anton (also known as "Dr. Jon") is the director of benchmark research at Purdue University's Center for Customer-Driven Quality. He specializes in enhancing customer service strategy through inbound call centers, and e-business centers, using the latest in telecommunications (voice), and computer (digital) technology. He also focuses on using the Internet for external customer access, as well as Intranets and middleware.

Since 1995, Dr. Jon has been the principal investigator of the Purdue University Call Center Benchmark Research. This data is now collected at the BenchmarkPortal.com Web site, where it is placed into a data warehouse that currently contains over ten million data points on call center performance. Based on the analysis of this data, Dr. Jon authors the following monthly publications: "The Purdue Page" in *Call Center Magazine*, "Dr. Jon's Benchmarks" in *Call Center News*, "Dr. Jon's Industry Statistics" in *Customer Interface Magazine*, and "Dr. Jon's Business Intelligence" in the *Call Center Manager's Report.*

Dr. Jon has assisted over 400 companies in improving their customer service strategy/delivery by the design and implementation of inbound and outbound call centers, as well as in the decision-making process of using teleservice providers for maximizing service levels while minimizing costs per call. In August of 1996, *Call Center Magazine* honored Dr. Jon by selecting him as an Original Pioneer of the emerging call center industry. In October of 2000, Dr. Jon was named to the Call Center Hall of Fame. In January of 2001, Dr. Jon was selected for the industry's "Leaders and Legends" Award by Help Desk 2000. Dr. Jon is also a member of the National Committee for Quality Assurance.

Dr. Jon has guided corporate executives in strategically re-positioning their call centers as robust customer access centers through a combination of benchmarking, re-engineering, consolidation, outsourcing, and Web-enablement. The resulting single point of contact for the customer allows business to be conducted anywhere, anytime, and in any form. By better understanding the customer lifetime value, Dr. Jon has developed techniques for calculating the ROI for customer service initiatives.

Dr. Jon has published 96 papers on customer service and call center methods in industry journals. In 1997, one of his papers on self-service was awarded the best article of the year by *Customer Relationship Management Magazine*.

Dr. Jon has published twenty-three professional books, and these are listed at <www.benchmarkportal.com>. Dr. Jon is the editor for a series of professional books entitled *Customer Access Management*, published by the Purdue University Press.

Dr. Jon's formal education was in technology, including a Doctorate of Science and a Master of Science from Harvard University, a Master of Science from the University of Connecticut, and a Bachelor of Science from the University of Notre Dame. He also completed a three-summer intensive Executive Education program in Business at the Graduate School of Business at Stanford University.

Dr. Jon can be reached at 765.494.8357 or at <DrJonAnton@BenchmarkPortal.com>.

Co-Author

Ad Nederlof is President and Chief Executive Officer of Genesys Telecommunications Laboratories, Inc. the leading provider of contact center solutions for Collaborative CRM.

Mr. Nederlof joined the company in February 1999 as Senior Vice President of the company's European, Middle East and African (EMEA) operations. Under Mr. Nederlof's leadership, Genesys' EMEA region achieved record results, growing revenues over sixty percent and changing the European organization from UK-centric to Pan-European. In February 2000 Mr. Nederlof became president & CEO of Genesys.

Before joining Genesys, Mr. Nederlof was President and Chief Operating Officer of Richter Systems, based in Atlanta, Georgia (U.S.) and Montreal (Canada). Previous to that position, he worked for Oracle Corporation, where he served as Vice President for Northern Europe with revenue responsibilities of more than $400 million. His career also includes years with Volmac Software Group (Cap Gemini) as Executive Vice President, and at ICL Netherlands, where he was National Sales Director.

Mr. Nederlof also served on the board of directors of Harbinger Corporation, based in Atlanta, Georgia, Business Information Group (BIG) in Utrecht, Netherlands, Lacys, based in Maarssen, Netherlands and at Exact software, based in DELFT, Netherlands.

Mr. Nederlof is the co-founder and shareholder of e-Novation group in Rotterdam, Netherlands. The group holds four companies: Lifeline Networks, e-Novation Portals, Cumquat Software, and Key-P Software.

Content Editor

Dr. Natalie Petouhoff (alias ,"Dr. Nat") is a principal investigator working with Dr. Jon Anton for BenchmarkPortal, Inc.

Dr. Nat's background ranges from technology to human resources. She has first hand experience at companies like General Electric, General Motors, Hughes Electronics, Universal Studios as well as Internet start-up companies.

For her outstanding work in technology at Hughes Electronics, Dr. Nat received three awards, namely: 1) the *Leadership Achievement Award* for leadership in the face of resistance, 2) the *Superior Management Award* for quick technology solution implementation with a tiger team, and 3) the *Peer-Selected Award* for demonstrating exemplary behavior towards peers.

Dr. Nat's formal education is in technology. She was awarded the General Motors Fellowship to complete her Doctorate of Engineering from UCLA where she did her thesis research at Oak Ridge National Laboratory and Hughes Research Laboratories in Metallurgy and High Energy Particle Physics. She also has a Master's and a Bachelor of Metallurgical Engineering degree from the University of Michigan, financed by five scholarships. This is her fifth book on technology and CRM.

Dr. Nat can be reached at (310) 314-4498 or at <www.LMRassociates.com> or by e-mail at <doctorofchange@earthlink.net>.

20:20 CRM A Visionary insight into unique customer contacts
The contact center is at the heart of many businesses today, and CRM initiatives are making customer contact even more critical to the health of every company. 20:20 CRM provides a strategic view of where businesses should be going with their customer contact operation, with practical examples of how to get there.
ISBN 0-9630464-5-4   By: Dr. Jon Anton and Laurent Philonenko   **Price: $24.95**

Benchmarking for Profits! BenchmarkPortal's Guide to Improve Your Contact Center, Your Career and Your Company
Done right, and done regularly, benchmarking provides improved work life, career advancement and substantially increased earnings on a consistent basis. This book is an essential manual for continuous improvement peer group benchmarking that shows convincingly why proper professionalism in today's environment requires benchmarking. Includes valuable information on how to benchmark through BenchmarkPortal and describes the latest products to help you get the most from this crucial activity.
ISBN 0-9719652-1-8   By: Bruce Belfiore with Dr. Jon Anton   **Price: $11.95**

Call Center Benchmarking "How 'good' is good enough?"
This "how to" book describes the essential steps of benchmarking a call center with other similar call centers, with an emphasis on "self assessment." The reader learns how to plan a benchmark, how to collect the correct performance data, how to analyze the data, and how to find improvement initiatives based on the findings.
ISBN 1-55753-215-X   By: Dr. Jon Anton   **Price: $39.95**

Call Center Performance Enhancement - Using Simulation and Modeling
This book provides its readers with an understanding about the role, value, and practical deployment of simulation - an exciting technology for the planning, management, and analysis of call centers. The book provides useful guidelines to call center analysts, managers, and consultants who may be investigating or are considering the use of simulation as a vehicle in their business to responsibly manage change.
ISBN 1-55753-182-X   By: Jon Anton, Vivek Bapat, Bill Hall   **Price: $48.95**

Customer Obsession: Your Roadmap to Profitable CRM
Finally, here is a book that covers the complete "journey" of CRM implementation. Ad Nederlof and Dr. Jon Anton have done the near impossible: to position CRM in such a way that it makes practical sense to C-level executives. Beginning with the title of the book, "Customer Obsession," on through the last chapter, this book positions CRM for what it really is, namely, a complete change in corporate strategy, from the top down, that brings the customer into focus.
ISBN 0-9719652-0-X   By: Ad Nederlof and Dr. Jon Anton   **Price: $24.95**

Customer Relationship Management: The Bottom Line to Optimizing Your ROI
Customer Relationship Management recommends effective initiatives toward improving customer service and managing change. Creative methodologies are geared toward building relationships through customer-perceived value instruments, monitoring customer relationship indices, and changing the corporate culture and the way people work.
ISBN 0-13-099069-8   By Dr. Jon Anton and Natalie L. Petouhoff   **Price: $33.33**

Customer Relationship Management Technology: Building the Infrastructure for Customer Collaboration

From our research on the American consumer, it has become very clear that potentially the best customer service strategy is "to offer every possible channel for the customer to help themselves, i.e., self-service." Customer actuated service is mostly driven by technology, and the "art" of self-service is to ensure that the technology is intuitive, easy to use, and that the customer is rewarded for "having done the job themselves." This book delves into all the technology solutions that enable self-service. The reader will find a robust description of the technology alternatives, and many examples of how self-service is saving companies money, while at the same time satisfying customers.

ISBN 0-9630464-7-0   *By Dr. Jon Anton and Bob Vilsoet* **Price: $39.99**

Customer Service and the Human Experience: We, the People, Make the Difference

One of the leading challenges for today's managers is the training and motivating of excellent agents. While much attention has been focused on the technology and benefits of providing multiple channels for customer contact, little attention has been paid to handling the human part of the equation—training CSRs to field more than just telephone communications. Great statistics and benchmarking help the customer service/call center professional keep ahead of the ever-changing business environment as the authors successfully blend the critical human aspect of the center with the ever growing need for metrics and the bottom line.

ISBN 0-9719652-7-7   *By Dr. Rosanne D'Ausilio and Dr. Jon Anton* **Price: $34.95**

Customer Service at a Crossroads: What You Do Next to Improve Performance Will Determine Your Company's Destiny

By consistently delivering information about products, services and information to customer service agents, based on their individual skill levels—at the right time in the right way, organizations are also delivering a consistent, clear understanding of corporate objectives and vision. The result: thousands of customer interactions that delight the customer and improve retention as well as corporate profitability. Optimizing agent performance can quickly deliver incredible returns beyond customer loyalty. That is what this book is all about.

ISBN 0-9719652-6-9   *By Matt McConnell and Dr. Jon Anton* **Price: $15.95**

e-Business Customer Service: The Need for Quality Assessment

With the advent of e-business technology, we suddenly find ourselves with completely different customer service channels. The old paradigms are gone forever. This books details how to measure and manage e-business customer service. The book describes the key performance indicators for these new channels, and it describes how to manage by these new rules of engagement with specific metrics. Managing customer service in this "new age" is different, it is challenging, and it is impossible to migrate from the old to the new without reading this book.

ISBN 0-9630464-9-7   *By Dr. Jon Anton and Michael Hoeck* **Price: $44.00**

From Cost to Profit Center: How Technology Enables the Difference

This book is a series of case studies in which we collected performance metrics before and after implementation of specific technology solutions for call centers. In each case study we saw varying levels of improvement, and were then able to quantify the financial impact in terms of ROS, and in some cases, in terms of earnings per share. For call center managers contemplating the addition of new call center technology, this book will be an asset in better understanding the impact of technology in enabling higher performance.

ISBN 0-9719652-8-5   *By Dr. Jon Anton and R. Scott Davis* **Price: $44.95**

Also Available from The Anton Press

THE
ANTON
PRESS

How to Conduct a Call Center Performance Audit: A to Z
Call centers are an important company asset, but also a very expensive one. By learning to conduct a performance audit, readers will be able to understand over fifty specific aspects of a call center that must be running smoothly in order to achieve maximum performance in both efficiency and effectiveness of handling inbound customer calls.
ISBN 0-9630464-6-2   *By Dr. Jon Anton and Dru Phelps* **Price: $34.99**

Integrating People with Process and Technology: Gaining Employee Acceptance of Technology Initiatives
This book contains valuable information regarding the "people" side of technology initiatives. Many companies buy the best hardware and software, and spend thousands of dollars implementing technology only to find out that the employees resist the changes, and do not fully adopt the new, and possibly, improved processes. By understanding how to manage people during change, managers will see a much quicker ROI on their technology initiatives.
ISBN 0-9630464-3-8   *By Jon Anton, Natalie Petouhoff, & Lisa Schwartz* **Price: $39.99**

Listening to the Voice of the Customer
With the help of this book, the professional skills you need to measure customer satisfaction will lead you to different approaches until you have found the one that best fits you, your company, and your organization's culture.
ISBN 0-915910-43-8   *By Dr. Jon Anton* **Price: $33.95**

Managing Web-Based Customer Experiences: Self-Service Integrated with Assisted-Service
The time to grow your call center into a multi-channel customer contact center is now. This book has the power to help you increase customer satisfaction through the implementation of Web self-service. The value of this book can be calculated in terms of calls deflected from your call center, increased customer retention, an ultimately in a healthy return on your investment. In this book, the authors take you step-by-step through the best practices that lead to a successful self and assisted-service strategy.
ISBN 0-9719652-4-2   *By Dr. Jon Anton and Mike Murphy* **Price: $35.95**

Minimizing Agent Turnover: The Biggest Challenge for Customer Contact Centers
Some agent turnover can be functional, but most turnover is dysfunctional and can be very expensive. This book explores the types of turnover, including internal versus external; and documents the typical causes of agent turnover. Most importantly, this book describes a methodology for diagnosing the root causes of your agent turnover, and suggests improvement initiatives to minimize agent turnover at your customer contact center.
ISBN 0-9630464-2-X   *By Dr. Jon Anton and Anita Rockwell* **Price: $39.99**

Offshore Outsourcing Opportunities
For call center executives wanting to explore and understand the benefits of offshore outsourcing, the authors have brought together 'under one cover' a comprehensive guide that takes the reader through each step of the complex issues of outsourcing customer service telephone calls to agents in another country. With the pressure of today's competitive climate forcing companies to take a hard look at providing higher quality customer services at lower costs, this book is a "must read" for every call center executive.
ISBN 0-9719652-3-4   *By Dr. Jon Anton and John Chatterley* **Price: $34.99**

Also Available from The Anton Press

Optimizing Outbound Calling: The Strategic Use of Predictive Dialers
The content of the book is organized in such a way as to assist the reader in understanding the complete end-to-end process of automated outbound call dialing. Specifically, the reader will find the following steps described in detail: a) preparing a needs assessment, b) selecting and contracting a predictive dialer supplier, c) implementing a predictive dialer solution, d) applying change management principles to ensure "buy-in" by existing agents, d) handling and using dialer reports, and finally, e) benchmarking dialer improvements to ensure attaining the anticipated ROI.
ISBN 0-9719652-2-6   *By Jon Anton and Alex G. Demczak*   **Price: $39.99**

Selecting a Teleservices Partner: Sales, Service, and Support
This book tackles one of today's hottest topics: Customer Contact Outsourcing. Companies are in a quandary about the myriad of teleservices questions they're faced with, such as deciding to outsource, cost / benefit analysis, RFP development, proposal assessment, vendor selection, contractual requirements, service level performance measurement, and managing an ongoing teleservices relationship. With the authors help, readers will find this complex issue straightforward to approach, understand, and implement.
ISBN 0-9630464-8-9   *By Jon Anton and Lori Carr*   **Price: $34.99**

The Four-Minute Customer: Getting Jazzed about Your People and Quality Management in Your Call Center
This is a very unique book directed at developing and maintaining "Top Reps" that are uniquely motivated to deliver the highest possible quality of caller customer service at your center. Learn what it takes to find and lead the best of the best. Don't settle for mediocrity. Instead, learn how to manage the best in class customer contact center by attracting and keeping Top Reps at your organization.
ISBN 0-9630464-1-1   *By Michael Tamer*   **Price: $34.99**

Wake Up Your Call Center: Humanizing Your Interaction Hub, 3ʳᵈ edition
With new and up-to-date material, this third edition speaks volumes about the need to reinforce the human element in the equation. This is a straight forward guide for humanizing the impersonal, with practical to-do's, real life examples, and applications to delight your customers. In depth chapters include mixed messages, change and stress management, conflict resolution, rapport building, and communicating powerfully, just to mention a few.
ISBN 1-55753-217-6   *By Rosanne D'Ausilio, Ph.D*   **Price: $44.95**

Order Form

Secure online ordering is available at: www.benchmarkportal.com/bookstore

Billing Information:	Shipping Information (if different):
Name	
Company	
Address	
Address 2	
City/St/Zip	
Phone	

Please charge my: ____ **American Express**   ____ **Discover**

                        ____ **Mastercard**   ____ **Visa**

Card Number

Expiration Date

Signature

I've enclosed a check in the amount of

Purchase Order Number

Book Title	Amt*	Qty	Total
Books Total			
Shipping and Handling			
For all U.S. addresses, $5.00 for the first book, $3.00 for each additional book.			
For all International addresses, books must be **pre-paid** and must include a shipping and handling charge of $25.00 for the first book and $10 for each additional book.			
Total Amount Due**			

*Call for volume and pre-order discounts available (805-614-0123 Ext. 10)

**State sales tax will be added where applicable

For other books, tapes, and videos visit our online store:

http://www.benchmarkportal.com/bookstore

Send all orders to:

BenchmarkPortal, Inc.

3130 Skyway Drive, Suite 702

Santa Maria, CA 93455-1817

For quick service, fax your order to: (805) 614-0055

For questions about your order, please call: (805) 614-0123 Ext. 10

INDUSTRY REPORTS

Industry Reports Available From BenchmarkPortal, Inc.

Secure online ordering is available at:
http://www.benchmarkportal.com/bookstore

or call (805) 614-0123 Ext. 20

These industry reports contain hundreds of call center benchmarks and best practices for a specific industry:

Aerospace

Airline

All Industries

Automotive

Banking

Brokerage

Cable Television

Catalog

Computer Hardware

Computer Products

Computer Software

Credit Card

Financial Services

Government & Non-Profit

Healthcare Provider

Help Desk

Insurance

Insurance – Health

Insurance – Life

Insurance – Property & Casualty

Outbound Teleservices

Publishing & Media

Retail

Technical Support

Telecommunications

Transportation

Travel & Hospitality

Utilities

Wireless

SERVICES AND PRODUCT LISTING

Services and Product Listing from BenchmarkPortal, Inc.

We provide several options to allow executives to choose the level of service that will optimize their return from the benchmarking exercise.

1. Self-Service Basic Benchmarking

Sign up at our Web site and talk to one of our customer service representatives. Your data can be entered securely online. Detailed, confidential reports showing your competitive performance are e-mailed to you within days of data completion and validation.

Recommended for: All call centers. Centers that do not have sufficient analytical staff are encouraged, but not required, to use a Purdue-certified consultant (see Web site) to help them with data gathering and report interpretation. Centers with their own analytical staff should consider sending us their specialist to receive training in the proper use of our benchmarking reports.

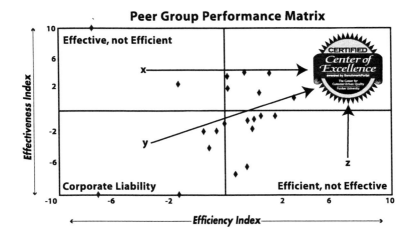

2. Competitive Benchmark Studies

Managers may want to a) see additional metrics that are specific to their sector; and b) know that the peer group is composed of their direct competitors. BenchmarkPortal is the trusted research organization that collects the additional data from all parties and produces the sector-specific report. ONLY anonymous and aggregate data are included as peer information in the reports.

Recommended for: Operations that are part of an identifiable competitive peer sector and that have key performance metrics that are specific to that sector.

3. Echo™ - 'Every Customer Has Opinions...even if no one asks™'

"With Echo, we now incorporate the 'voice of the customer' into everything we do. We love it."
— Joyce Whalen, eBay Director of Customer Experience

BenchmarkPortal introduces a groundbreaking new approach for translating direct customer feedback into rich business intelligence. *Echo ™* incorporates the best practices from 'world-class' companies based on our own extensive benchmarking studies.

Echo ™ challenges the traditional approach to measuring and improving service. The status quo has consistently fallen short of delivering results. Based on our research, we have taken the best practices of the best companies and incorporated them into a dynamic closed-loop approach that really delivers.

Echo ™ provides an all-in-one solution:

- Scientifically-based customer feedback collection
- Primary source for monitoring agent effectiveness
- Service recovery, including post-recovery effectiveness
- Core cause determination and analysis
- Effective, behavior-based agent coaching
- Meaningful metrics to track results
- Real-time Reporting
- Business intelligence needed to make informed decisions

We can help you develop and implement our revolutionary monitoring and coaching approach without loss of precious time in confronting technology and implementation issues. In most cases, we can launch *Echo ™* in just 60 days.

Hello.
I used to be your best customer.
I had to repeat my name over and over. Do you even know me?

Every time I called, you transferred me to someone else.

I spent a lot of money with your company. But I never felt very important.

You kept trying to sell me something I told you I didn't need.

I got a better offer from your competition. Now I'm their customer.

4. Fair-Compare™ Agent Satisfaction Benchmarking

 Finally, BenchmarkPortal introduces a new benchmarking option designed specifically for Contact Centers ...a method to compare the satisfaction results of your Contact Center agents to other Contact Center agents!

As a Contact Center Professional, you know the importance of retaining your talent. Our **Fair-Compare**™ benchmarking surveys and reporting system quickly pinpoint areas of risk to proactively resolve them.

Fair-Compare™ lets you compare your Contact Center agents based on any category captured, including:

- Tenure
- Age-range
- Job Title
- Skill-set
- Supervisor
- And lots more!

Fair-Compare™ provides the ability to compare your Contact Center results to:

- Your Peer Group
- Your Industry
- Best-in-Industry
- Your Demographic Region
- Similar Environments

Customizable, always available, Online Reporting is a central feature of **Fair-Compare**™, providing results that you can act on quickly. Survey results help you pinpoint exact areas to focus on for immediate improvement initiatives, giving you the "Why" behind each "What".

Use the results from your **Fair-Compare**™ **Agent Satisfaction Benchmark** to:

Promote Your Contact Center as an Employer-of-Choice!

5. Contact Center Assessment

Dr. Jon Anton directs an on-site, in-depth assessment. Result is a 100+ page, point-by-point report on all key performance indicators, complete with color graphics. Can be performed on a collaborative basis with the client's consultants.

Recommended for: Cost and performance-minded managers who:

- want a baseline status (especially if new to the job)

- desire a serious analysis of operational performance and financial impact (ROI and EPS)

- are considering outsourcing (cost-benefit analysis)

- require qualified due diligence assistance in mergers and acquisitions.

6. Contact Center Site Certification

Managements who want their centers to be certified as best-in-class have urged us to develop this program, which utilizes our database, expertise and proprietary performance indices.

Recommended for:
- Best practices organizations

- Outsourcers

- Overseas operations of U.S. based organizations

7. AT&T College of Call Center Excellence

AT&T College of Call Center Excellence provides training courses that result in certification of personnel.
Courseware is available for managers, supervisors and agents. Courses are taught both in-person and online. Some courses are in conjunction with BenchmarkPortal industry partners.

Recommended for: All centers. Training is a budget item for all centers that is rarely optimized. We can help you to get more for your training dollar.

8. Benchmarking 201: Your Competitive Edge

This NEW hands-on workshop is for all call center professionals who need a sound benchmark methodology to audit current performance results, then prioritize solutions toward achieving a competitive ROI. Participants will calculate the cause/cost of poor/excessive performance by case studies and quantify a 30-day impact plan. Attendees earn Certification as a Benchmark Specialist through Purdue University's Center for Customer-Driven Quality.

What Will I Learn?

- **Benchmarking the Difference**: Satisfaction, Retention, Operations, Cost containment

- **Competitive Performance**: Peer Reports, Gap analysis on effective/efficiency metrics

- **Solutions Savings**: Root Cause impact, Simulation charts, quantifiable action plan

Recommended for those who need a Peer-Industry Benchmark

a new way of thinking

Contact Centre Solutions

Listening to your customers –
your success depends on it

In the last decade, "call centres" have evolved to "contact centres" managing all types of customer transactions using all types of media, not simply the telephone.

Whether a large, intricate company department or a single business unit, a contact centre's business objectives and goals are the same:

- Productive personnel who handle customer transactions promptly and competently to assure customer satisfaction and enhance customer loyalty.

- Efficient use of resources and technology to control costs and increase profits.

Contact Centre Solutions is a TELUS portfolio that offers advanced customer contact management products and services. We have become one of the leading providers of flexible and scaleable contact centre solutions, operating some of the most sophisticated contact centres in North America. Linked by state-of-the-art technology and processes, we are operated and supported by a team of more than 6,500 specialists.

In 2003, the Contact Centre Solutions team transformed their offerings into a cohesive, all-encompassing market approach with service offerings across the entire continuum of client requirements.

In 2003, the Contact Centre Solutions team transformed their offerings into a cohesive, all-encompassing market approach with service offerings across the entire continuum of client requirements.

TELUS®
the future is friendly™

a new way of thinking

Listening to your customers – your success depends on

Our services include:

- Consulting services
  - Current technical assessment/review and recommendations
  - Benchmarking & migration studies
  - Strategic business consulting

- Contact centre management
  - Contact queuing
    - Skill-based routing
    - Multimedia routing
  - Reporting
    - Real time and historical

- Technology optimization
  - Computer telephony integration (CTI)
  - Advanced desktop applications
  - Advanced speech applications

- Performance optimization
  - Workforce management
  - Quality management

- Knowledge optimization
  - Information management
  - Case management
  - Customer relationship management (CRM)

- Intelligent voice and data network

- Customer self service
  - Self service voice (IVR)
  - Self service data (Internet)
  - Speech technologies (speech recognition, voice verification, text-to-speech)

Contact Centre Solutions

:LUS Contact Centre Solutions offer the most innovative and flexible anagement options in the industry. Solutions can be packaged in any ombination of premised-based or hosted to suit the clients' unique usiness needs.

Client premised based

Hosted contact centre solution

Blended solution (client premised based with strategic outsourcing)

ur solutions are predicated on the recognition that clients can be at fferent stages of the technology evolution in their contact centre rategy and delivery. We also appreciate that there are various chnology, management processes and training issues which need to ork in concert for maximum business benefit.

nis understanding has led to our affiliation with best-in-class vendors, aking it possible for us – at TELUS Contact Centre Solutions – to ddress and meet an extensive range of business needs.

Our solutions are predicated on the recognition that clients can be at different stages of the technology evolution in their contact centre strategy and delivery.

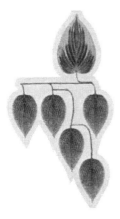

"Finally a book that clarifies CRM (customer relationship management). Learn everything you need to know to implement a successful and profitable CRM strategy at your company. I strongly recommend you read this book to better understand CRM and its potential impact on your customers and your company's bottom line."

- *Natalie Avery*
Customer Service CRM Center Manager

"CRM is the new craze at companies large and small. Everyone wants to better manage their valuable customer relationships. Finally here is a book that really does 'connects all the dots' and makes sense out of the 'what, when, and how' related to CRM. I strongly recommend this book for anyone involved with CRM initiatives."

- *Colleen Kifner*
Franklin Consulting Group
866-FC-GROUP
crkifner@aol.com